A Theology of Literature

A Theology of Literature

The Bible as Revelation in the Tradition of the Humanities

William Franke

CASCADE *Books* · Eugene, Oregon

A THEOLOGY OF LITERATURE
The Bible as Revelation in the Tradition of the Humanities

Cascade Books
An Imprint of Wipf and Stock Publishers
199 W. 8th Ave., Suite 3
Eugene, OR 97401

www.wipfandstock.com

PAPERBACK ISBN: 978-1-5326-1102-5
HARDCOVER ISBN: 978-1-5326-1176-6
EBOOK ISBN: 978-1-5326-1175-9

Cataloguing-in-Publication data:

Names: Franke, William.

Title: A theology of literature : the Bible as revelation in the tradition of the humanities / William Franke.

Description: Eugene, OR: Cascade Books, 2017 | Includes bibliographical references.

Identifiers: ISBN 978-1-5326-1102-5 (paperback) | ISBN 978-1-5326-1176-6 (hardcover) | ISBN 978-1-5326-1175-9 (ebook)

Subjects: LCSH: Bible as literature. | Religion and literature. | Revelation in literature. | Humanities.

Classification: LCC BS535 F6 2017 (print) | LCC BS535 (ebook)

Manufactured in the U.S.A.   06/29/17

To Hans Ulrich Gumbrecht

Contents

Preface and Acknowledgments

THIS BOOK BEGAN DECADES ago with my studies in theology at Oxford University. I have borne the Bible in mind ever since as an unsurpassable model of the revelatory potential of literary art while I continued over many years as a professor of comparative literature to study and teach literature at universities around the world. I dedicate the book to one of my own teachers in comparative literature, one who showed particular interest in my discerning the modes of theology as implicitly operative in supposedly secular literature. He understood and credited my discovery of literary form as a kind of religious revelation, as heretical as this seemed to be for the profession of literary criticism and theory in the secular milieu of the university.

My thanks also to Northwestern University Press for permission to adapt this reflection on the Bible from the opening chapter of *The Revelation of Imagination: From Homer and the Bible through Virgil and Augustine to Dante* to a more diversified audience, including confessional readerships beyond the walls of the academy. The Bible is many things to many people. Criticism and scholarship—together with speculative thinking—concerning the Bible can appeal to our human quest for understanding and insight at very different levels. My reflection on the literary premises of revelation in the Bible reads very differently depending on the diverse socio–cultural contexts—with their respective mindsets—into which it is projected. This reflection has become quite a different sort of disquisition and inquiry in the process of adaptation and expansion.

My symmetrical thanks, therefore, are due to Cascade Books for according this literary-critical and scriptural meditation the opportunity to travel into circles that it would otherwise never reach, and in particular to Christian Amondson for his initiative and invitation. The entire text has been reworked and further elaborated in this transition, and it contains several wholly new sections as well. Two of these sections, the discussions of Psalms and of Job, had to be left out of the original chapter on the Bible in *The Revelation of Imagination* because of space but are now included. The Introduction and Conclusion were written for this book alone and contain new formulations concerning the Bible's relation to literature. They treat specifically—and speculatively—the question of literature as a form of theological revelation.

The book adapts, with permission, materials appearing in earlier redactions in the following publications:

1. "From the Bible as Literature to Literature as Theology: A Theological Reading of Genesis as a Humanities Text." *Interdisciplinary Humanities* 29.2 (2012) 28–45.

2. "The Exodus Epic: Universalization of History through Ritual." In *Universality and History: The Foundations of Core*, edited by Don Thompson, Darrel Colson, and J. Scott Lee, 59–70. Lanham, MD: University Press of America, 2002.

3. "Prophecy as a Genre of Revelation: Synergisms of Inspiration and Imagination in the Book of Isaiah." *Theology* 114.5 (2011) 340–52.

4. "Writings and Revelation: Literary Theology in the Bible." *Theology and Literature* 28.4 (2014) 1–16.

5. "Gospel as Personal Knowing: Theological Reflections on not Just a Literary Genre." *Theology Today* 68.4 (2011) 413–23.

6. *The Revelation of Imagination: From Homer and the Bible through Virgil and Augustine to Dante.* Copyright © 2015 by Northwestern University Press, Published 2015. All rights reserved.

From the Bible as Literature to Literature as Theology

WHAT IS A THEOLOGICAL reading of the Bible, and what is a literary reading? The intricate dance of different methods of reading has become dizzying in recent decades in the wake of important advances—but also of devolutions and deconstructions—in critical theory. We are frequently faced with a crisis of confidence in language, with the collapse of belief in its ability to deliver any sort of authoritative truth. Yet, at the same time, we also encounter ample evidence of the discovery of language's unlimited, infinite—and some would even like to say "divine"—poetic potential.

Traditionally, biblical interpretation strives to preserve some core of theological meaning that remains intact regardless of the variety of its literary forms. The approach taken here reverses this strategy. The literary form of the Bible, far from being definitively framed as the opposite of its theological content, can move into the position of representing the truly revelatory element that enables this unique book to communicate an authentic presence of divinity. Literary form, when appreciated to the full extent of its creative, world–disclosing capabilities, can become intrinsically revelatory in a sense that deserves to be recognized as deeply and truly theological. Figurative language and story-making, among other literary resources, open meaning without limits and in so doing open a horizon of the infinite that allows for and invites being understood theologically.

Further complicating and sometimes bedeviling the issue are various types of secularization of theology that have gained currency in the modern era and are present and powerful now on the contemporary scene of culture. These in turn are contradicted by theological radicalizations of diverse sorts spanning different world views and crossing major geopolitical and cultural divides. Still, between the extremes of militant secularism and religious fundamentalism, the literary and the theological poles interact, challenging one another reciprocally to reach out toward realization of their highest aspirations in some incomparably provocative and potentially life-changing ways.

Formerly, the discourses of literature and theology could be held apart and distinguished in clear, uncontaminated terms. But it has become more and more difficult not to see quintessentially literary modes such as metaphor and narrative as always already implicated in any theological pronouncement, whether descriptive or prescriptive, dogmatic or speculative. On the other side of the equation, it has also become more difficult not to see the infinite openness of poetic language as a dimension that calls for interpretation in theological terms. Its endlessly malleable figurative and rhetorical means are all too well-adapted for intimating something about the unfathomable origins and inscrutable ends of the world and of life as a whole. This unlimited "theological" dimension dwelling in the Logos—in language and literature as such and as creative of sense—resides not so much in what language specifically says, its semantic and propositional contents, as in its forms of expression and their ineluctable structural openness.

Literary expression, as inherently poetic, is uncircumscribable and remains infinitely open to unlimited creative makings and re-makings of sense. Almost any utterance considered from a specifically literary point of view seems capable of endlessly different meanings in an unlimited range of further contexts that would embrace, ultimately, everything imaginable. Moreover, this comprehensive scope and universality can hardly be denied a far-reaching theological import. Such a creative Logos performs as an implicit account of the whole of things and of their origin. Just such an account is what theology traditionally has provided in explicit terms, with its narrative line stretching from alpha to omega, Genesis to Apocalypse.

The upshot of these developments is that the older practice of reading the Bible as literature has gone through a remarkable "conversion" into reading literature as theology. We now not only look for literary motifs and forms that are deployed within the theological frame of the Bible and are adapted to its revelatory purposes: we can also recognize revelatory powers at play specifically in the Bible's literary forms themselves as framing and informing its religious contents and determining the sense of its theology.

The previous way of reading the Bible as literature, in spite of the Good Book's self-attributed status as theological revelation, as "the Word of God," remained under the authority of the academy working as an organ of our secular society. Reading the Bible as literature served the function of effectuating a secularization of sacred literature so that it could be read without "belief" and independently of confessional allegiances. Thus it was made appropriate for "general education" in the public schools and in universities. But in our now arguably post-secular age, the reverse has become possible: we can read even secular literature by self-consciously human artists as having a potentially sacred power and significance. This sea change has brought about a kind of apotheosis of literature now appearing in its full intensity and purport as revelation—even, in some cases, as manifestly theological revelation.

This transgressive "transfiguration" fundamentally changes our understanding of what theology is or can be, as well as metamorphosing our notion of literature. The transition now underway in the mutually transforming interaction between literature and theology is being encountered today in some particularly self-reflective modes in the fields of Religion and Literature and of Dante Studies (two of my own areas of scholarly specialization). But it can also have considerable impact on our way of reading the Bible itself.

The "theology of literature" that I have previously developed in a variety of works situated in different disciplinary matrices and in diverse publishing contexts concerns sacred Scripture as much as secular religious literature; indeed, it can be brought to bear first and foremost on our understanding of the Bible. The aim and purpose of the book in hand is to put forward this way of reading the Bible in the aftermath of what I view and explicate elsewhere as a revolution in the theory of literature in our time.

Bibliographical Note to Introduction

A sense of the current crisis of theological language and a sampling of some of the quandaries it has produced for religious institutions can be garnered from Christopher Spinks, *The Bible and the Crisis of Meaning*. Northrop Frye famously discussed "The Crisis of Language" generated by challenges to biblical literalism in *The Double Vision: Language and Meaning in Religion*, chapter 1. A good introduction to the "post-secular" is Douglas and Rhonda Hustedt Jacobson, eds. *The American University in a Postsecular Age*, 3–15.

The designated "sea change" as it applies to Dante studies, sounding poetry in its depths as theology, is made into something of a manifesto in *Dante's Commedia: Theology as Poetry*, edited by Vittorio Montemaggi and Thomas Treherne. It is pursued further by Montemaggi in *Divinity Realized in Human Encounter: Reading Dante's Commedia as Theology.*

Regina Schwartz's work—notably her edited volume *The Book and the Text: The Bible and Literary Theory*—pioneers passages between secular criticism and biblical scholarship. Amos Wilder, *The Bible and the Literary Critic* also deserves mention as highly influential in opening this orientation and path of inquiry. The state of the art is well represented by *Literature and the Bible: A Reader*, edited by Jo Carruthers, Mark Knight, and Andrew Tate. Current approaches to teaching the Bible as literature are explored in "Rethinking the Bible as Literature: A Pedagogical Forum Edited by Emily A. Ransom with Peter Hawkins," *Religion and Literature.* The Bible's extensive impact on literature in English is surveyed in *The Blackwell Companion to the Bible in English Literature*, edited by Rebecca Lemon, Emma Mason, Jonathan Roberts, and Christopher Rowland.

Lastly, I would place several of my own previous books, including most recently *Secular Scriptures* (2016), likewise in this dawning horizon for the broad field of religion and literature, in which secular literature shows up as transfigured by the light of theological revelation. One place where I address the designated revolution in literary theory of recent decades, in which criticism itself can become something of a (mediation of) revelation, is in "Literature as Liturgy and the Interpretive Revolution of Literary Criticism," the Appendix to Chapter 3 of *Poetry and Apocalypse: Theological Disclosures of Poetic Language* (151–58). See also below, in this volume, Chapter 2, section III: Creation by the Word—Theory and Theology.

CHAPTER 1

The Bible's Place in the Tradition of the Humanities

I. Word of God Become Flesh

CERTAIN DISTINCTIVE QUALITIES OF knowledge in the humanities were understood more profoundly, or at least more intriguingly, in antiquity and the Middle Ages than they are today. This applies particularly to the knowledge conveyed through literary texts. The nature of such knowledge has in some ways been obscured through the scientific approach of modern philology to textual analysis. With the rise of modern empirical science as the dominant paradigm for knowing, texts taken as specimens for analysis are dissected according to the will and criteria of a knowing subject considered to be wholly external to them. Previously, it was possible for the text to exercise sovereign authority in determining its own meaning and in interrogating the reader and potentially challenging the reader's insight and very integrity.

Bound up with this sovereignty, the poetic text was capable of assuming a theological aura. This is most evident and explicit in the case of the Bible as paradigmatic text. However, before the secularist turn of culture in modernity, certain other literary texts, too, were attributed a quasi–prophetic authority and revelatory power. They were treated as authoritative sources of an event of truth in a sense that we are now in a position to recover thanks to what can be called the "post-secular" turn of postmodern culture.[1] Part of my purpose in what follows is to develop for interpreting the Bible an approach freed from secularist dogmas that reduce texts to inert objects for our examination, thereby exorcizing their authoritative voices and preempting their ability to speak to us and so to structure the encounter with the reader in their own way. This approach can be extended from the Bible to humanities fields and literature more generally.

I carry out such extensions to other books most programmatically in *The Revelation of Imagination*. Rather than understanding the humanities as some lesser kind of science, a clumsy application of scientific method to a more recalcitrant sort of material, I propose to understand the whole liberal arts curriculum (which traditionally included the language arts of grammar, rhetoric, and dialectic, but also the quantitative sciences of geometry, arithmetic, astronomy, and music) from the point of view of the humanities. Seen from this angle, liberal learning in science and arts alike shows up as driven by the human interests that motivate all search for knowledge. Such knowledge, moreover, as is clearest in the case of the knowledge gained through humanities texts, turns out always to be in some way self-knowledge—which entails above all a knowing of one's own limits and of one's place in the overall scheme of things. This is what used to be called "wisdom"—or, in the Latin humanist tradition, *sapientia*.[2]

Taken as reflecting on ourselves, humanities texts are not objects of scientific analysis so much as partners in dialogue. If this is so, then their meaning must change over the course of history, for it depends essentially on how they are read by diverse readers who exist in changing historical contexts. Reading is a process of projection, of finding oneself and one's human concerns in the world projected by the text, as well as of mapping

1. Post-secularity has been discussed intensively in theology and philosophy, for example, in Phillip Blond, *Post-secular Philosophy: Between Philosophy and Theology* and more broadly in Jolyon Agar, *Post-Secularism, Realism and Utopia: Transcendence and Immanence from Hegel to Bloch*. Charles Taylor's *A Secular Age* and Jürgen Habermas's *An Awareness of What Is Missing: Faith and Reason in a Post-Secular Age* inform much recent discussion. Concerning specifically the Bible, the crucial historical transformations leading up to this shift are outlined by Hans Frei, *The Eclipse of Biblical Narrative*. Closer to where we are today, Walter Bruggemann, *Texts Under Negotiation: The Bible and Postmodern Imagination* analyzes as "postcritical" the current situation in biblical interpretation.

2. I make this argument more extensively in "Involved Knowing: On the Poetic Epistemology of the Humanities" and also in the Introduction to *The Revelation of Imagination*.

the text's concerns onto one's own world of experience.[3] Even if the text, as a sequence of markings, stays literally the same, humanity or the individual reader, the other partner in the dialogue, undergoes continual change. The text's meaning changes, accordingly, with each new interpreter and with each new era of interpretation, and this mobility belongs to its own internal life and structure. The dimension of reading, taken as intrinsic to the text, lends it its dynamism and its living significance.

The Bible is arguably the most eminent example of this life-process inherent in a work that is passed down from generation to generation.[4] It embodies the relationship of Israel to its past and to its tradition not as an artifact available for objective analysis but as a partner in dialogue.[5] The Bible, moreover, presents itself as a dialogue between divinity and human beings interpreting their common life as a response to God's calling. There is thus also an explicitly theological frame for the "dialogue" within the Bible between numerous different phases and strata of a people's history. This history extends far beyond biblical times and indeed all the way to our own contemporary world, since in each period the dialogue has to be renewed on the basis of new situations and sensibilities, both within faith communities themselves and in their broader cultural contexts.[6] This history must always be appropriated anew in every age in order to achieve its full meaning. Only so may it truly be said that the Word "became flesh and dwelt among us" (John 1:14).

This majestic and quite astonishing phrase has specific doctrinal meaning when read in the context of particular confessional communities, such as churches, but it also announces a general interpretive principle: the meaning of tradition is experienced only in its application to life in the present. This application is carried out by countless communities in

3. Paul Ricoeur theorizes this process in his general *Interpretation Theory*, as well as specifically with regard to the Bible in *Figuring the Sacred* and in *Essays on Biblical Interpretation*.

4. Masterly substantiation and illustration is provided by Pietro Boitani, *Ri–scritture* (translated as *The Bible and its Rewritings*); and James Kugel, *In Potiphar's House: The Interpretive Life of Biblical Texts*.

5. Walter Reed's approach to reading the Bible as literature turns specifically on its dialogical character. See his *Dialogues of the Word: The Bible as Literature According to Bakhtin*.

6. Reflection on world-wide variation of readings over time is proposed by *La Bible: 2000 Ans de Lectures*, ed. Eslin. Further intra- and extra-biblical perspectives are found in *Die Bibel im Dialog der Schriften: Konzepte intertextueller Bibellektüre* (translated as *Reading the Bible Intertextually*) eds. Alkier and Hays.

different contexts and, in the end, also by single individuals. Individuals must appropriate the words of Scripture—make them "flesh" and give them a meaning in terms of their own lives.

As the "Word of God," therefore, the Bible provides a uniquely privileged model for humanities texts, specifically for their establishing a dialogue with the reader, the one to whom they are addressed. The very notion of the book as such—as authoritative, as not just an object among objects but as circumscribing and transcending them, and as the voice of Truth—is intimately bound up with the example of the Bible and with the influence it has exerted down through the ages. In religious and in secular spheres alike, the Bible is somehow not on the same level as other books. And yet the Bible, as a "great book" in this tradition of texts, and as embodying a revelation of truth living in history through reinterpretation in continually changing contexts, is exemplary of what holds for the rest as well: we can and should learn to read other great books of imagination as revelatory in a similar sense. This book, proverbially *the* Book, is absolutely fundamental not only to religion but also to the whole secular tradition of Western humanities. That tradition is itself exposed in its light as far from purely secular. And reciprocally, divine revelation in the Bible, rather than being lost or denied, shows up in this more widely diffused light as concretely and compellingly realized through its endless worldly transmogrifications as interpreted from age to age and across cultures.

II. The Ongoing Process of Translation as a Dialogue Among Cultures

Despite its authoritativeness, this imposing book, perhaps more than any other, has undergone continuous transformation. In the first place, this is so because the Bible is deeply enmeshed in the process not only of linguistic but also of cultural translation. To begin with just the linguistic level, it is without question the most translated of all books. It has been translated into virtually every written language, as well as being the object of an endless succession of different translations into the same language, as in the case of English.

Translation into English, which has been continuous from Anglo-Saxon times, began to approach familiar forms with the work of William Tyndale in the early 1500s. This translation, together with other sixteenth-century translations, like Miles Coverdale's and the Geneva

Bible, became the basis for the translation commissioned by King James I of England known as the Authorized Version (1611). Widely accepted as standard, it was at various times revised, and by the nineteenth century, when earlier manuscripts had been discovered and numerous errors of translation detected, a revision was undertaken that produced the Revised Standard Version.[7]

Even more importantly, translation in a cultural sense is constitutive of the ongoing tradition of the Bible. Such cultural translation, in effect, is undertaken already within the Bible itself, signally by Saint Paul, who says that he became all things to all men so that by all means he might save some (1 Cor 9:22). Indeed the Bible is not, like science, cast into mathematical language that is the same for all everywhere. The Bible, by its very nature, speaks into the particular historical situations of individuals and their specific cultures, tailoring its message to what they are ready to receive and understand. This phenomenon is already reflected internally to the work itself again by Paul in his preaching to the Athenians as recorded in the Acts of the Apostles.

Paul begins by citing the Greek philosophical conception of God's unknowability as expressed in the inscription "TO THE UNKNOWN GOD" that he happened to see on an altar in the city as he was being led to the Areopagus by philosophers who were eager to have this "babbler" explain his strange new doctrine. Against their avowed ignorance, Paul proclaims the self–revelation of God in Christ: "Whom therefore ye ignorantly worship, him declare I unto you" (Acts 17:22ff). Paul casts his message in terms that answer to and challenge the Greeks' philosophical culture. He works from their admission of the vanity of their search for "the Unknown God." Indeed, God remains an unknown to the intellect alone. But shifting the ground out from under them, Paul affirms that the one true God who is hidden from the highest reaches of human intellect has revealed himself in history—specifically in the messianic event of Jesus the Christ, in his death and resurrection for the salvation of the world. Paul's speech is thus conscious of itself as a humanities text in exactly the sense I have been at pains to define: its meaning depends on and must be adapted to how it can

---

7. The process of revision has continued further. Nevertheless, I prefer to draw quotations from the Authorized Version for the most part because its memorable phrasing and resonant diction have indelibly stamped the English language and its literature. The tensions and pressures bearing on this sinuous history are sifted by Alister E. McGrath, *In the Beginning: The Story of the King James Bible and How It Changed a Nation, a Language, and a Culture.*

be received and interpreted by its hearers, who change and will continue to change on an ongoing basis into the future.

This outward-reaching, self-transforming character of the Bible is not to be taken for granted. Another "great book" of monotheistic religion, the Qur'an, is characterized precisely by its *un*translatability. In principle, the message of Islam can be communicated only in Arabic. The Name of God—*Allah*—cannot be properly spoken in any other language. In the faith tradition it spawned, the Qur'an is held typically to be a purely divine revelation that was given whole and intact to Mohammed without any human mediation. Read in this way, the Qur'an repels attempts to interpret it in terms of its history and to examine its process of formation. It is deemed to be forever unchanging in form as well as in content and is to be learned and recited verbatim, even by students who do not understand Arabic and so cannot interpret its meaning.[8]

The Bible, in contrast, comes to us swaddled in a complicated and fascinating history of composition, one that needs always to be unraveled and that continues to be woven as the book continues to be interpreted in new historical situations. At the base of it all are the Hebrew Scriptures, the sacred books of Israel, which are in themselves already a whole library of diverse kinds of literature: τα βίβλια means literally "the books." They are traditionally classified as Law, Prophecy, and Writings, but these are only the most general categories into which the Bible's varied component books break down.

III. Translating the Past into Living Tradition

All these Scriptures, which to Jesus of Nazareth were sacred—indeed, the Word of God—were taken over by his followers and reinterpreted as alluding to and culminating in the Christ event. This event's beginning with the birth from a virgin was interpreted, for example, as the fulfillment of the prophecy of Isaiah 7:14: "Behold, a virgin shall conceive, and bear a son, and

---

8. The broad contrast drawn here, relaying current prejudices, would require, of course, qualification and scholarly refinement considering the diverse currents within Islam, for which see Lenn E. Goodman, *Islamic Humanism*. Let me also stress that my crude attempt to mark a difference between the Bible and the Qur'an in their relation to history is not a value judgment. It does not mean to detract from the mystical beauty or the prophetic power and truth of either work. I would further add that we, in Western societies, have everything to learn from the different approach to revelation in Muslim tradition that we still know far too scantly.

shall call his name Immanuel." This interpretation is often held, however, to be erroneous in linguistic terms, since the word "parthenos" (παρθένος) or "maiden" in the Greek translation of the Bible, the Septuagint, which is quoted by Matthew 1: 22–23, translates Isaiah's Hebrew word "'almah," which means simply "young girl." Luke 1:27 also calls Mary a virgin, but he too is working from the Septuagint, and so it seems that the whole story might just have been generated by a mistranslation.

Yet the issue is not nearly so simple, since the "original" Hebrew text is itself reconstructed from the Masoretic text, which dates only from the sixth century AD and was finally established by Aaron Ben Asher as late as AD 925. The discovery of the Dead Sea Scrolls in 1947 has shown that the Greek Septuagint (third century BC) may occasionally be even closer than the Masoretic text to these more ancient versions of the Hebrew Scriptures. Moreover, many earlier glosses on Isaiah also understood him to be prophesying a virgin birth. There was thus an ancient tradition that formed the basis for the Septuagint translators' understanding "'almah" to mean "virgin." The term has evidently shifted in meaning over time and may, after all, have originally connoted virginity.[9]

A wider, remoter background, moreover, in ancient Near Eastern comparative mythologies and fertility cults can also be discerned as bearing on these terms and has been alleged to motivate this doctrine at least sub-consciously.[10] David Tacey treats "The Myth of the Virgin Birth" for its symbolic and spiritual value and takes its significance at this level as counting against its literal-historical sense.[11] This inference is not necessary, in my view, but I agree about refusing the tendency to take the literal too literally or simply as plain fact unfiltered by interpretation of any kind, since the literal sense, too, especially in narrative, needs to be understood as itself a symbolic way of signifying.[12] Even literalness can prove true and be experientially verified only in and through the relationships that it makes possible and fosters.[13] It is known only in and through being lived—of which the ways are myriad. For Meister Eckhart, an actual virgin birth of the Christ

9. Brown, *The Birth of the Messiah*, 143–53.

10. Warner, *Alone of All Her Sex*.

11. Tacey, *Religion as Metaphor*, 87–105.

12. Bal, *Loving Yusuf*, distinguishes between "literalism," of which she is a "strong advocate," and "fundamentalism," which in appealing to "an immutably referential, prescriptive meaning" fundamentally misconstrues "how signs work" (4).

13. Again, I defer to my "Involved Knowing: On the Poetic Epistemology of the Humanities."

child in the intimacy of the human soul is experienced as a miracle at the core of awakening to mystical union with God.[14]

The prophecy of a virgin birth testifies, in any case, to a belief deeply rooted in the early Christian Church that plays itself out in the Christian appropriation of Jewish Scripture. The Christian communities began developing a literature of their own openly centered on Christ, who was interpreted as the foundation stone: "the stone that the builders rejected has become the corner-stone" (Ps 118:22). The narratives of the life of Christ—the Gospels—became the foundation stone of the New Testament. Building upon the Hebrew Scriptures (*Tanakh*), this ensemble of books was based explicitly on the revelation of God in Jesus of Nazareth. A new overarching meaning was thereby lent to the Hebrew Scriptures, taken as the Old Testament, within the architecture of the Christian Bible.

Jesus in the Gospels steps forth as an interpreter and renewer of the revelation of the Hebrew Scriptures. He affirms continuity with this tradition as the bedrock for his revolutionary message in the Sermon on the Mount: "Think not that I am come to destroy the law, or the prophets: I am come not to destroy, but to fulfill" (Matt 5:17). But he also, in the same speech, underlines the rupture of his own words with tradition: "Ye have heard that it was said by them of old time. . . . But I say unto you. . . ." Precisely this process of reinterpretation from within constitutes the backbone of biblical tradition. And, in this respect, the Bible provides an especially revealing model for humanities texts as continually in the process of rewriting themselves. This follows inevitably from their being intrinsically addressed to a reader: they thereby establish a dialogue between the reader's present and what has been handed down from the past.

The far-reaching significance of the Bible's translatability resides in the inexhaustibly productive and *re*productive potential of this book as a literature that can be lived. It interprets human experience by the light of divine revelation, which is itself in every instance a humanly situated idea with unlimited different possible meanings.[15] This will be demonstrated in different ways by selections from the Bible exemplifying the imaginative

14. Among other places, in a cycle of Sermons for Christmastide (*Predigten*, 101–4), Eckhart elaborates his doctrine of the eternal birth of the Son in the virgin soul of every believer.

15. Some newly emerging, "postmodern" possibilities for construing the Bible's status as "revelation" and its claim to "inspiration" are explored in relation to traditional disciplines such as biblical studies and church history by Terrence E. Fretheim and Karlfried Froehlich, *The Bible as Word of God in a Postmodern Age*.

genres of Myth, Epic History, Prophecy, Apocalyptic, Writings, and Gospel. Each new genre develops creative forms that incorporate and build upon its predecessors in constructing the overall revelation through imagination of the designated "divine Word."[16]

Pursuant to recent revolutions in literary theory, in which the very possibility of meaning has been seen to be generated by the differential nature of the linguistic sign, "revelation" can newly be understood as a poetic no less than a religious category. In some crucial respects, these two types of revelation might well be construed as overlapping or even sometimes as coinciding with one another. Rather than considering literary form to be extraneous to religious content and considering the linguistic medium to be purely instrumental to conveying a revelation of transcendent meaning, it has become imperative to apprehend the content of the form and to explore poetic form's own intrinsic capacities and propensities to deliver a revelation that might well be considered to be theological in the sense most pertinent for many types of readers today. The present monograph aims, in its own speculative way, to reflect on a constellation of literary genres within the Bible and to demonstrate in new ways their aptness for communicating something of what has traditionally been held to be divine revelation. The properly literary resources of these genres prove to be constitutive of religious revelation as it is actually experienced.

This ongoing interpretation of human experience through the shifting lens of revelation in tradition is played out in exemplary fashion from the very beginning of the Bible. Genesis proffers an interpretation of the meaning of the cosmos and of humanity's place within it. Genesis 1–2 does this particularly in the form of myth, the myth of Creation. The significance of this myth is disclosed anew in each succeeding historical period as a result of contact with new situations that bring out relative constants of human experience from novel angles and in new relations.

16. A very different reflection on the literary genres of the Bible, but one that is also leveraged from the theoretical innovations of comparative literature, is proposed by David Damrosch, *The Narrative Covenant: Transformations of Genre in the Growth of Biblical Literature*.

CHAPTER 2

The Genesis Myth:
Existence as Revelation

I. The Archetypal Dimension of Significance

THE PREVAILING LITERARY GENRE of Genesis, at least in the primeval history or prehistory contained in the stories of Creation, Fall, and Flood (chapters 1–9), is myth—μύθος in Greek, which means literally "word," "speech," or "story." I use the word "myth" neutrally as a description of literary type or genre and absolutely without prejudice as to the actual or possible truth of its contents. I consider myths specifically as stories that objectify fundamental conditions of existence and interpret their human significance. Genesis may be about something that happened in the past to certain individual human beings who lived and died long ago, but it is also about a universal condition that belongs to us all. The narrative invites us to interpret ourselves as being created in God's image—and also as fallen away from the original, ideal perfection of our being. In interpreting Genesis as "myth," we discover its narrative to be not only about what happened "once upon a time," "in the beginning," but also about what is a reality for us today.

Genesis is about essential conditions of existence as we experience them in everyday life. These conditions are embodied in imaginative form in its narratives. Humankind and the human condition are represented symbolically as a particular individual named "Adam." This becomes the name for humanity as a whole, first as it exists in its original, perfect, intact state, and then as fallen. The technique employed here by the Hebrew imagination is to represent the whole human condition concretely as a particular individual, the first: Adam. Adam serves as Archetype of the human race. Myths are necessary forms of expression for existential realities of this order. They are found in the analogical imagination of primordial cultures the world over. Especially where faculties of abstract thought have not yet developed or become dominant, the general significance of human existence cannot be expressed except in such a symbolic language.

What, according to biblical revelation, is the nature of the relation between God and humanity, between humanity and nature, between man and woman? The biblical doctrines on these matters are embodied in the vivid scenes of Genesis 1–3, which are not *only* about one individual—Adam, by name. His very name tells us that they also refer to the whole human race: "Adam" in Hebrew is the common noun "man," *'adam*, used as a proper name. This clearly is the way St. Paul understood it in fashioning what became a normative doctrine for Christian churches. The foundation for the notion of original sin that was to be developed later by St. Augustine was laid down by Paul through his interpretation of Genesis 3: "Wherefore, as by one man sin entered into the world, and death by sin; and so death passed unto all men, for that all have sinned . . ." (Rom 5:12). The universality of Adam's sin for Paul corresponds to, and seems to be made necessary by, the universality of Christ's act of redemption: ". . . death reigned from Adam until Moses, even over them that had not sinned after the likeness of Adam's transgression, who is the figure of him that was to come. . . . For if by one man's offence death reigned by one; much more they which receive abundance of grace and of the gift of righteousness shall reign in life by one, Jesus Christ" (Rom 5:14–17). Paul reads Adam's sin as universal in order that Christ's resurrection may also count as a universal cosmic event redeeming all humankind (1 Cor 15:20–23).

The doctrine of original sin often constitutes a stumbling-block for modern readers, who typically find it to be repugnant. It arouses the furor of believers and non-believers alike because of the seemingly blatant injustice and illogicality of holding all humans responsible and burdening them with guilt for the sin of one man. But if the contingent, precarious existential condition of all humans is symbolized in Adam—a condition inducing them to wish to be autonomous, lords of themselves, no longer subject to any higher authority than their own—then Adam's sin stands for a predicament that inevitably affects us all. As finite creatures, we are not self-sufficient. Our condition is one of dependence, of subjection to biological and psychological needs, and of conscious, indeed anxious awareness of them to boot.

We are determined, furthermore, as ambiguously within and at the same time above nature, and as gendered. All this is also represented in the Genesis account of a man who needs a companion but cannot find one among the animals that he is given to name. And this condition is intimately bound up with our susceptibility to sin. We sin, fundamentally, because we would like to evade our condition of dependency and its attendant deficiencies so as to be like God—indeed *be* God—that is, be perfectly self-sufficient, autonomous Lords of our own lives, not to mention those of others.

Our dependent, vulnerable condition leads us into temptation, furthermore, by luring us into not respecting the divisions upon which the whole order of Creation is based—from the moment God banishes chaos by separating the light from the darkness, the waters that are above the firmament from those below it, the dry land from the sea, etc. Our ever renewed attempts to transgress the limits set to man—to "become like gods, knowing all," in the serpent's words of temptation to Eve—are all prefigured in the first, the archetypal human sin. A little later in the narrative, the building of the Tower of Babel again expresses a failure to accept the separation of heaven from earth, a separation upon which the creation is founded. Refusal to accept the human condition and its limits—in other words, the human desire to be and to supplant God—is exposed as the universal root of sin. It is repeatedly represented in narrative form in the first eleven chapters of Genesis, as well as throughout the rest of the Bible—sometimes in more explicit, less mythic modes. The disease of a will in this way tending to transgress the boundaries set for it by its Creator constitutes an original sinfulness—or rather a *disposition* to sin. This wayward, insubordinate will is itself the constitutive corruption of human nature that is engendered by Adam's sin—or that, more exactly, is objectified mythically *as* his sin.

Our purpose here is not to unravel the theological conundrums of the doctrine of original sin but simply to recognize Genesis as an interpretation of the universal meaning of human life, first as created in its original, ideal perfection, and then as it actually exists in a fallen state. In the interpretation of existence in Genesis, all creation is ordered to and dependent on God: it is as it pleases Him that it should be. This is affirmed and reaffirmed in the refrain "and God saw that it was good," which rings repeatedly through the narrative. Moreover, according to this account of Creation, humanity is its crowning glory. Standing in direct and privileged relation to God as made in his own image, the human being is a sort of delegate who is sovereign in turn—God's viceroy, who is granted dominion over the earth. This, at least, is *one* of the interpretations that the Bible offers of human beings' place in creation, the one suggested particularly by Genesis 1 and taken up in lyric form in Psalm 8, which places humans "a little lower than the angels," with all other created things "under their feet."

There is another, in some ways quite different interpretation given in the second chapter of Genesis. This second account is anthropocentric. It *begins* with the creation of man, whereas in Genesis 1 humanity is created at the end of a series of six days of Creation. In Genesis 2, moreover, Creation is effected not by the word, as in Genesis 1 ("And God *said*, Let there be light," etc.). In Genesis 2, man is created rather by being molded from the earth, the way clay is molded by a potter, making for a much less hieratic, more naturalistic account of man's origin. This diversity generates a dialectic of views about the human condition already within the first two chapters of Genesis. Woman is portrayed in Genesis 2:20-25 as created after man, as springing derivatively out of his side. In contrast, in Genesis 1, woman is the symmetrical mirror image of man and is created together with man in the image of God: "So God created man in his own image, in the image of God created he him; male and female created he them" (1:27). Together these accounts may reflect the experience of woman as man's spiritual partner and peer, when not his adversary—as fully his equal by nature but also, at the same time, institutionally and socially, subordinate.[1]

If this were a science text, we would expect it to tell us unequivocally the facts about what happened "in the beginning." But in reading it as a humanities text, we are interested not so much in what it says, truly or falsely, about a remote past as in what it says about relationships in which we participate presently. The failure to make this distinction has fed raging controversies in the history of interpretation of the Bible centered typically upon this Creation story. However, Creation may have happened, in fact and in detail, once upon a time, Genesis communicates a wealth of understanding concerning the human condition—and thereby of *self*-understanding potentially valid for us still today. The Bible, as a humanities text, thus asks

1. See Robert Alter, *The Art of Biblical Narrative* for this suggestion and others helpful to the reading offered here. Also highly illuminating is Leon R. Kass, *The Beginning of Wisdom: Reading Genesis*, who reads the story as a philosophical anthropology interpreting our human and sexual nature.

to be read not just as a document about what happened in time past but as a word and, moreover, a "truth" living in the present, "the word of life." It becomes even, in a sense, by dint of constant reinterpretation and renewal, a word of "eternal" life—as in Peter's confession to Christ: "thou hast the words of eternal life" (John 6:68). Hence the necessity of translation and re–translation—and of re–interpretation and re–appropriation—in order that its truth take root and germinate in each new culture and individual life with which it comes into cross–fertilizing contact.

Whether or not Genesis is a factual account of what happened "in the beginning," we need to give a practical priority to the significance of the relationships represented in it—for they still obtain, in ever evolving form, today and at any time—rather than just to purportedly historical facts pertaining exclusively to the past. The Bible has always been understood in relation to the human contexts in which it is lived and relived; for this reason, it is newly discovered, interpreted, and applied in every new present.[2] In this crucial respect, it represents an essential paradigm for humanities texts as vital negotiations between past sedimentations of culture and social pressures in the present. Precisely this type of interaction between the ages produces continual innovation—and occasionally continental shifts—in the history of interpretations.

II. Layers of Tradition in the Creation Story

Tensions and contradictions in the Creation story emerge when we ask questions such as, What is the sequence of creation? Is man created last, after the lower orders of the animals and as the crowning glory of creation, or first, before them all? What about woman's creation? Is she made together with man, symmetrically in a single act, or after him, and indeed after the other animals are brought first to Adam to be named? Where is man created, inside the Garden or outside of it? By what means is Adam created? Is he uttered into existence simply by the divine Word or is he formed out of the dust (*adamah*) of the ground into which life is breathed?

The apparent incompatibilities between these, at any rate, differing accounts compel us, following well over a century of critical scholarship on the Bible, to distinguish between several different traditions and even to conjecture different documents whose accounts have been woven together

2. This emerges strikingly from later literary recreations such as those inventoried by David Jasper and Stephen Prickett, *The Bible and Literature*, 65–79.

in the Creation story as it now stands. We can distinguish two stories right away, one in chapter 1, in which the six days of creation culminate in the creation of man and woman together simultaneously, and the other in chapter 2 (starting from verse 4), in which Creation focuses on and practically begins with man. In this second account, the other creatures are made first after man, and woman is then made out of a rib taken from his side by God, who has put him into a deep sleep. As analyzed by scholars, the Creation story in Genesis is thus already a composite of antecedent traditions. This supposition makes it possible to explain a number of inconsistencies between the first two chapters by distinguishing various strata of the Creation story as composed in different times and places by different authors expressing distinct theological visions.[3]

Genesis 1, read as a humanities text in the mythic mode, has a vision of its own: we must attempt to discern what it is saying about the significance of the universe and of human life. Its distinctive style already tells us a great deal. The numerically measured, cadenced unfolding of the event over seven days is embodied in a formulaic language enriched by constant repetition and refrains ("And God said . . . and it was so"; "And the evening and the morning were the first . . . the second . . . the third day," "And God saw that it was good"). Such rhythmically repeated refrains magnify the glory of Creation as a harmoniously appointed, ceremonious composition. The sense of a decorous procession in stately parade of all things in order, according to their kinds, is conveyed by the even, paratactic syntax, in which phrase after phrase begins with "and," giving each statement full and equal dignity. This writing is organized by parallel clauses saturated with repetitions that are cumulative and of graduating intensity. The chapter is, in effect, a solemn celebration of Creation wrought in a grand literary style. The successive presentation in a series of seven days leading up to the Sabbath makes the Creation itself a kind of liturgy, the first of all time, replete with blessings and directives for prospering ("And God blessed them and said unto them, Be fruitful and multiply and replenish . . ."). The universe

3. A classic formulation of this "source–critical" hypothesis dates from Julius Wellhausen, *Prolegomena zur Geschichte Israels* (1878). Specific hypotheses concerning documents are still very much in question in Biblical scholarship. The model I evoke is based on Martin Noth, *Überlieferungsgeschichte des Pentateuch* (1948), translated as *A History of Pentateuchal Traditions*, and used, for example, by Antony F. Campbell and Mark A. O'Brien, *Sources of the Pentateuch: Texts, Introductions, Annotations*. This heuristic model helps to isolate a few fundamental differences in the handling of ostensibly the same stories. A useful introduction is Richard Elliot Friedman, *The Hidden Book in the Bible: The Discovery of the First Prose Masterpiece*.

is a temple of God, with the moon and sun as its lights, the greater light to rule the day and the lesser light to rule the night.[4]

This hieratic vision of the Creation in Genesis 1 belongs, appropriately enough, to a strain of the Genesis tradition that is attributed by scholars to priestly writers presumably at Jerusalem. Numerous scholars place it during the captivity in Babylon in the sixth century BC. This magnificent panorama highlighting the Creator's sovereignty and the perfect order and coherence of the Creation would undoubtedly have been inspiring and reassuring for a people living in distress and exile. It would be a tribute to the creative splendor and resilience of their faith even during times of severest tribulation. Other scholars have placed it earlier, even as early as the ninth century BC. In any case, given its Priestly origin, the document used by the final editor of Genesis as we have it in this opening chapter has been labeled by scholarship as the "P document."[5]

Compared with this priestly version of Creation and its exalted, sacralizing cosmogony, the account in chapter 2, which continues with the story of the Fall in chapter 3, is more earthy in character. It describes man as molded by God from the dust of the ground. It is assigned by some scholarship to the so-called "J document," supposed to have originated in Judah in the period of the divided kingdom (922–722 BC). Its various parts were identified, in the first instance, by their reference to God as Jahweh (Yahweh, or better: YHWH), sometimes transliterated as *Jehovah*. This distinguished it from the "E document," supposed to have been composed during the same period, but in the northern kingdom of Israel (also called "Ephraim") before its fall to the Assyrian empire in 722 BC. Furthermore, in this document, God is referred to as *Elohim*, a form

---

4. This description, absorbing traditional interpretations of Genesis 1–3, is guided by Robert Alter's magisterial reading of the two different biblical Creation stories in *The Art of Biblical Narrative*, 142–47.

5. This so-called documentary hypothesis has again become a subject of considerable scholarly controversy and has, since the upheavals of the 1970s, often been declared to be no longer believed. See, for example, *Abschied vom Jawisten: Die Komposition des Hexateuch in der jüngsten Diskussion*, eds. Jan Christian Gertz, Konrad Schmid and Markus Witte. However, much recent scholarship marks a swing back towards accepting it in modified forms. Richard Elliott Friedman, *The Bible with Sources Revealed: A View into the Five Books of Moses* assembles evidence in its favor. Mark McEntire, *Struggling With God: An Introduction to the Pentateuch*, 11–24, and J. N. Aletti and J. L. Ska, eds., *Biblical Exegesis in Progress* confirm that the documentary hypothesis leaves many open questions and disputes but in any case remains influential as a model for understanding the Bible's composition.

of the generic word for God (*El*), presumably in the belief that God had been designated by his proper name (YHWH) only since the revelation to Moses (see Exod 6:2–3).

In the J account of Creation, we find ourselves in the midst not of a liturgical ritual but of a materially imagined encounter with an anthropomorphic God. Somewhat clumsily concrete, the "voice" of the Lord "walks" in the garden in the cool of the day (3:8). In this author's vision, moreover, humanity remains close to nature rather than in a position of domination over it. Man is formed out of the dust of the ground and is animated by a physical breathing into his nostrils of the "breath of life" rather than being created purely by the word and in God's immaterial "image." Man has, furthermore, a clear function binding him to the earth: he is supposed to till the ground. He is placed in the Garden "to dress it and to keep it" (2:17). This account is more natural and less ritualized. Its language reflects not the formal balance and symmetry of the cosmos, as in the bird's-eye view of Genesis 1, so much as the complex interweave of the world as seen from within and below. Materials and motivations mix in the dense opacity of a mysterious life and inscrutable destiny marked by the inexplicable catastrophe of the Fall from perfection. The predominantly "hypotactic" syntax, complicated by subordinate clauses beginning with "before," "but," "when," "for," "then," is dense and ramified, branching out and twisting round: it contorts the orderly, evenly measured flow of the "paratactic" syntax (and . . . and . . . and) that rhythmically scores chapter 1.

The closer relation with nature goes hand in hand with a somewhat more childlike relation to God. In the first version of Creation, as already suggested, Man is its crowning glory and represents God within it, whereas in the second version man is a weak creature in need of help and in mostly passive roles, as when he is put to sleep so that a rib may be taken out of his side and be formed into his female counterpart. Also, not the abstract, ideal symmetry of "male and female created He them" (1:27), but an apparent derivativeness of woman from man—Eve emerging out of Adam's side—is graphically embodied in their physical origins. God himself, in this version, is closer to nature and humanity, acting like a potter molding clay to create man instead of as a spirit moving over the water and creating solely by his divine Word. The whole account is more anthropocentric: the Creation is seen *not* vertically from above, in a sovereign panoptic vision that can survey all levels of the universe, but rather from the level of the ground and from the point of view of man on the earth.

Like the P document, the J document is conceived of as a strand that extends further and can be detected running all through the book of Genesis and indeed throughout the whole Pentateuch. It is readily recognizable by its vivid, concrete, bodily imagination of human life and its anthropomorphic conception of God. The divine and the human are not quite completely separate in J's mythical depiction of the era of the giants, the *Nephilim* (Gen 6:4), who are produced by the sons of God mating with the daughters of men. The mythic proportions of the lifespan of the patriarchs descended from Adam, several of whom, like Methuselah, live to be over 900 years old, make them into people unlike us, for whom a mere seventy years, "three score and ten," is the common measure (Ps 90:10). The J author, moreover, is often wildly unpredictable and enigmatic. It is J who writes, "Enoch walked with God; and he was not, for God took him" (5:24). The divine mystery impersonated in the unaccountable character of Yahweh is full of exuberance and blessing and also of "terrifying extravagances," such as the attempt upon Moses's life by God himself (Exod 4:24). J delivers an uncanny narrative full of irony and paradox.[6]

The J account also displays to particular advantage the concreteness of the Hebrew language and consequently of the thought it expresses always in terms of physical phenomena such as bodily organs and functions. For example, the word *ruah* for "spirit" derives from the word for "wind" (Gen 1:2) or for "breath" (Ps 104:30; cf. also Jer 34:14). Intellect and emotion both have their seat in the "heart" (*lev*), as in the phrase: "and every imagination of the thoughts of his heart was only evil continually" (Gen 6:5). This contrasts with the faculties of abstraction in which the Greek language excels, and which it uses for conceiving intellectual essences such as the soul. The physical immediacy of the Hebrew language guides the J writer into dense regions of inextricable confusion riddled with all the contradictions of terrestrial existence.

We see, then, that the two different—howsoever complementary—stories say some rather different things about the significance of the cosmos and human life. The one highlights the symmetrical orderliness of creation seen from God's point of view, while the other envisages the concrete, corporeal involvement of human life in a natural environment rather than just in a symbolic order: it exposes complex nexuses of causation and the moral

---

6. For a provocative hypothesis on the J writer, see Harold Bloom's commentary and introduction to *The Book of J*, translated from the Hebrew by David Rosenberg. Quotation, 317.

dilemmas that they entail. This diversity illustrates how humanities texts from the beginning inevitably produce—and are produced by—the diverse meaning for different interpreters of facts that are humanly significant. Significance is inevitably manifold because human beings are many and diverse, and the significance of things can never be clearly abstracted from these concrete individuals and the particularities of their existence. The different—and in some respects incompatible—accounts of Creation in Genesis 1 and 2 might seem problematic if we take them as factual accounts of a unique historical event. Read as humanities texts, on the other hand, they testify to the rich variety and contradictoriness of human experience itself in its evolving metamorphoses.[7]

In the narratives of Creation, Fall, and Flood, various ways of understanding human existence are embodied in objective form. Particularly poetry, with its figurative objectifications, is apt to express human experience of the relations between humanity and God, humanity and nature, man and woman. One of the cardinal principles for the interpretation of humanity offered in Genesis is the idea of sin. As it is portrayed in the primeval history comprised in chapters 1 through 11 of Genesis, before the ancestral history that begins with the call of Abraham in Genesis 12, sin consists fundamentally in usurping upon God's authority. It is first committed when humans disobey the commandment not to eat of the fruit of the tree of the knowledge of good and evil, which allegedly makes one "like God, knowing good and evil" (3:5). It is through not respecting the divisions that constitute the very order of Creation that evil comes about once again when the mixed marriages between the sons of God and the daughters of men engender giants and, as a result, violence in the earth (6:1–7). Sin thereby emerges as a transgression against the clear separation of humanity from divinity. By wanting to be "like God," humans collapse the fundamental divisions on which Creation, as described in the first chapter of Genesis, is erected.

Creation itself is conceived basically as the use of language for making distinctions. All the verbs for creating in Genesis 1:1–5, of which God is the subject, have this sense: created, divided, called, said. Creation is essentially a system of verbally instituted differences. The attempt of mortals to lift themselves up to the height of God, dramatized in the original sin of

7. A good sense of the shifting multivocity of meanings accreting around the opening chapters of Genesis in the interpretive tradition can be acquired from Elaine Pagels, *Adam, Eve, and the Serpent* and Gary A. Anderson, *The Genesis of Perfection: Adam and Eve in Jewish and Christian Imagination*.

Adam and Eve eating the apple, so as to become "like gods," is repeated in the construction of the Tower of Babel. Here it is the power of the word—at least of a unified word intelligible to all—that is taken away from humanity as punishment and as surety of their keeping to the subordinate place assigned them in the order of Creation. The word, at the same time, is also the power by which humanity and everything else is created. It is the word that enables humans to participate in community with God and to share in the divine life. However, the word also transcends humanity and can even be taken away from them (or be turned into an unintelligible babble), if they do not respect the transcendent authority on which it is grounded.

III. Creation by the Word—Theory and Theology

In addition to its pivotal role in Genesis in the Hebrew Bible, the motif of Creation by the Word also forms the starting point for Christian revelation in the Gospel of John: "In the beginning was the Word [ὁ Λόγος], and the Word was with God, and the Word was God. All things were made by him [the Word], and without him was not anything made that was made" (1:1). The word is thereby given a metaphysical status as the origin and cause of all that is. Thematically, language is the bridge between God and Creation, just as formally the language of Genesis embodies the order by which and in which God creates. In its symmetry and progressiveness, the narrative of Creation incarnates and in some sense even institutes the order of Creation itself.

Creation by the Word offers a warrant for believing that the natures of things are ultimately revealed by their verbal interpretations. The word interprets the being of the thing it names. The passage describing Creation recognizes the constitutive role of language in the very making of the world. Language is not merely an adventitious, extra something supervening upon a world fully determined in its ontological constitution already before and without respect to the advent of language. Instead, all that exists is called into being by the Creator Word. Humanity's being made in God's image expresses itself particularly in Adam's possessing speech and using words to name creatures, thereby echoing God's use of the Word in Creation. The animals are brought to Adam "to see what he would call them" (2:19). The originally divine faculty of naming is handed on to Adam made in God's image and establishes Adam's relation of dominion over the things of the world. It makes him a kind of co-creator. His creative use of this verbal faculty might even be taken as a means of expression and fulfillment of the divine injunction to Adam and Eve: "Replenish the earth and subdue it" (1:28).

Humanity rules and is productive on earth essentially by the power of the word—the very power through which God creates. We will focus recurrently throughout our investigation on how humanity's relation to the world in its origin and essence is embodied in an act of naming that exercises and releases a divinely creative power over things. This is a power, however, that transcends humanity and is subject to greater powers of creation than its own—powers that humans can only attempt to correspond to and mirror or mediate. This is one level of insight that the inherently linguistic and literary viewpoint of humanities studies is especially apt to bring to focus and to foster: interpretation by the word is the means and the very medium of study in the humanities. Such study therefore finds a matrix in the story of Creation, where the word is revealed symbolically as instrumental to the very being and making of the universe.[8]

Crucial to our predicament today is understanding that the creative power given us especially through language, as the origin of human *techne,* is not just an arbitrary power to manipulate the world at will but is rather embedded within an overall order of Creation that surpasses us and that remains beholden to other and higher powers than our own will to dominate. Such is at least one vital lesson to be drawn from the Genesis text as applied in our contemporary context, given the unprecedented risks brought about by our all-too-uncontainable capabilities for manipulation of our biological environment and for the biomechanical reconstitution of our bodies as cyborgs with prostheses (including computers as extensions of our brains) and even of our very selves through gene technology. This might seem to be a purely secular reading of a literary text. However, there is arguably a kind of theological sense here as well simply in the acknowledgment of dependence on a higher power than human powers alone. This respect for an order of things beyond human making is an urgent message borne by Genesis as a humanities text in our apocalyptic times of the eclipse of

---

8. Literary-theoretical underpinnings of this revelation by the creative word are probed in David G. Firth and Jamie A. Grant, eds., *Words & the Word: Explorations in Biblical Interpretation & Literary Theory.* German-Jewish language philosophy is applied to the exegesis of Genesis 1–12 in a speculatively original fashion by Mendel W. Tronk, *Wesen und Ursprung der Sprache: Eine Untersuchung.* Leonard L. Thompson, *Introducing Biblical Literature: A More Fantastic Country* similarly emphasizes "the world–creating power of language" (5) revealed in the Bible.

nature and the destruction of the very conditions of life through unbridled exploitation by human technology and industry.

Theology, in the sense intended here, is not a set of doctrines given in advance and circumscribing the meaning assigned to the text but rather an inherent dimension of the text itself in its humanly uncircumscribable potential to signify: such significance reaches beyond our will and even comprehension. This "theological" sense emerges as an uncontrollable and incalculable address coming from or through the text. As such, the text is allowed to challenge the reader and every method of reading, as well as to critique every context in which readers might wish to place it definitively, so as to control and contain it.

Theology, in this type of reading, is not imposed externally on the text. Instead, reading the text radically as literature opens up a theological dimension of transcendence beyond human control from within the text's own linguistic and imaginative fabric. Accordingly, reading the Bible theologically here means reading it non-dogmatically—as free of any particular, ecclesiastically normed interpretation, but equally as free from any secular norms. Our secular culture, too, is full of embedded doctrines dictating what texts and language and human subjects are supposed to be. These often unconscious notions can work as dogmatic prejudices that delimit what words are able to mean and do. The model of the Bible serves to alert us to this possibility that the word itself in the literary text might be allowed to speak in its intrinsically "theological" character as a word with infinite and open meaning—unconstrained by the limited capacities of any finite, intending subjects and their culturally specific hermeneutic apparatus.

What comes from the "text itself," of course, is received and assimilated variously into one's own world of culture and into one's personal vision of truth. Although the type of reading I practice in these pages gives authority to the text and even receives the text's own voice as "theological," my reading is nevertheless to be understood as belonging to the sort of philosophically-leveraged critical readings that have flourished in the wake of the new departures of literary theory in recent decades.[9] "Theology" functions here as a hermeneutic that can serve like structuralism or deconstruction, or psychoanalysis or feminism or Marxism, to define an overall

---

9. A good sampling of such theoretical approaches is presented by Regina Schwartz, ed., *The Book and the Text: The Bible and Literary Theory*. A rich, state-of-the-art harvest of literary theory and criticism as it applies to the Bible has been gathered together in Carruthers et al., *Literature and the Bible: A Reader*.

approach to the world, one which is integrated with how we understand texts and events and, more broadly, our "life-world."

Regina Schwartz suggests that, starting from the time of the Reformation, theology "went underground" for several centuries, in flight from scientific-historical criticism of the Bible, but that today "theology . . . is returning in the guise of theory."[10] Schwartz acutely assesses the Pandora's box opened by the new engagement of biblical studies with literary-theoretical discourse, noting that biblical history (including the issue of what history is) and biblical authority (including the authority of the text) can no longer be cordoned off from literary theory and its radical questioning of historicity and textuality as such. Our perception and understanding of the ways in which history and text may serve as vehicles of truth and revelation have been—and are being—challenged: they are being radically transformed through theory-influenced practices of reading and interpretation.

Previously, the historical-critical examination of the Bible, considered as scientific philology or research, was kept separate from matters of faith and theology, but such segregation is no longer possible in the face of the theory revolution that affects our approach to interpretation of texts and history and existence generally. Text and history no longer have any purely factual, non-theoretically inflected basis to stand on. The effects of this revolution make themselves felt with complete indifference to any disciplinary limits. As Schwartz lucidly recognizes, "questions of faith are matters of theory."[11] This implicit dependence of theology on theory—and vice versa, I would add, of theory on theology—underwrites the interdisciplinary and ultimately extra-disciplinary readings that I offer, putting forward a theory of humanities texts, exemplarily the Bible, as "theological" revelation. As a discourse on the Unconditioned and answering to no other master, theology—or, more precisely, the literary theology that I propound—is itself unconditioned by disciplinary limits. Particularly, as we are about to see, the ontology of history (what it *is*) is penetrated by theory—and therefore also by "theology" in the sense that this book defines; namely, discourse open without disciplinary divisions to the infinity of all possible relations. Word without end.

10. Schwartz, *The Book and the Text,* 12.

11. Ibid., 14.

CHAPTER 3

The Exodus Epic: History and Ritual

I. Defining a Literary Genre

READ AS RELIGIOUS MYTH, Genesis represents fundamental conditions of human existence in the form of a narrative about a couple of characters, Adam and Eve, who stand for the whole human race. Such interpretation of the "truth" of Genesis in no way precludes belief in Adam and Eve as having been real people, particular individuals—the first—but it maintains that the story, at any rate, also reaches far beyond them as single individuals in order to represent something about the universal condition of humankind. This, as we saw, is how St. Paul reads it: for Paul, in Adam "all have sinned" (Rom 5:12). Such an interpretation enables us to read Genesis as being not only about what happened in a remote past but also about us and our present relationships. We find ourselves exposed in this text as subject to certain factors—signally, freedom and its infirmity—that determine our being human. This human condition is embodied archetypally in Adam and Eve. Precisely in this sense, Genesis can be understood as belonging to the genre of "myth."

The Book of Exodus, on the other hand, can best be assimilated to another literary genre, namely, epic history.[1] An epic is the story of the origin of a people. It focuses on some founding event in which a people becomes

---

1. For epic as a genre, see Frye, *Anatomy of Criticism*, 315–26.

a cohesive group with a collective life and thereby constitutes itself as a nation. This event is memorialized in the nation's traditions and gives the people its sense of having an identity. The founding event of the nation, its heroic origin, furnishes it with an image also of its future destiny. The purpose for which a certain people came into being illuminates its national history as a whole and offers guidance for each step on the way toward fulfillment of the future promised in its beginnings.

In actual fact, a variety of traditions are likely to condense around any event that comes to be chosen as the unifying symbol for the origin of the nation. The Trojan War, as recounted by the Homeric epics, emerged in this way as the founding event of Greek national consciousness. The Greek world's ideals of human excellence and heroism were given a compelling imaginative representation by the Homeric epics that became normative for diverse Hellenic city-states and for the entire civilization which they spawned. Similarly, the Roman people's sense of a unique historical mission and even of a cosmic purpose was concentrated into the image of Aeneas as conqueror and founder that was cast by Virgil's *Aeneid* into enduring, monumental form. Chivalric poems such as *Beowulf* and the *Chanson de Roland* had a comparable function in defining a distinctive civilization for medieval England and France—just as did the *Niebelungen* in German-speaking lands and the Icelandic sagas in Scandinavia.

All these epics embody interpretations of idealized historical events that express the ethos of a nation. They tell what a certain people has been enabled to become through the actions of its heroes, as well as revealing proleptically what that people will be called to realize in the challenges facing it in the future. It is important to distinguish the language of myth from the language of epic so that the very different truth claims appropriate to each of these diverse genres can be discerned and respected and appreciated. Myth at its most proper and paradigmatic sounds deep, timeless, ultimately unanswerable questions like: Where did the universe come from? What is humanity's purpose in being here? Why is there suffering and death?[2] Epic history answers to another set of questions concerning not the general conditions of human existence but rather the historical identity of a people. What sets them apart from all other peoples of the earth? How did they come to band together in the first place? What are

2. This is not to deny or even to diminish the ideological determination of myth, which is effectively underscored by Bruce Lincoln, *Discourse and the Construction of Society: Comparative Studies of Myth, Ritual, and Classification.*

their distinguishing characteristics, their special virtues and talents, as well as their defects and weaknesses, their nemesis? What should they aspire collectively to achieve? While great epics very often enfold mythological cosmogonies and cosmologies, their specificity as epic demands to be understood in terms of the category of history and of the distinctive historical mission of a certain people.

What, then, is history? Of all that happens, those events become historical that leave a trace in the memory of a people because of their having significance for this people as a whole. "History" always consists in events being understood in accordance with a certain significance. But the "true" significance of events is recognized always only retrospectively: only in the sequel does the full meaning and purport of an event become manifest. Viewed from a historical distance, certain events take on value as emblematic and as standing for crucial junctures of a people's past. One event may even become a symbol for all the rest.

In a manner something like this, we might surmise, the Exodus became the founding event of the Hebrew nation. Indeed, the very name "hebrew" seems originally to have designated not so much an ethnicity as a social class, the lowest.[3] The Hebrews may not have been a distinct people at all prior to the Exodus event. To this extent, it is conceivable that the very existence of a Hebrew people may be more a result of the Exodus as the formative narration of the Hebrew nation than an independent and antecedent fact. This phenomenon of narrative proving instrumental in the production of nationhood has become more transparent to us through its modern manifestations, especially in postcolonial societies.[4]

The process of making a history, and through it a people, is exemplified by the way that, from among many memories, the Exodus emerged symbolically as the crucial founding event for the Hebrews.[5] Crossing the Jordan, conquering the Canaanites, victorious military campaigns against neighboring peoples, deliverance from invasions, and successful resistance in the face of foreign empires—these and other such scenarios became confirmations of God's special favor and tutelage of Israel as revealed originally and most powerfully by the Exodus. The Hebrews, both as individuals and in groups, experienced their God as a liberator and savior in manifold

3. See von Rad, *Theologie des Alten Testaments*, "Die Herausführung aus Ägypten," 189ff.

4. See particularly Bhabha, ed., *Nation and Narration*.

5. Cf. Martin Buber, "Holy Event (Exodus 19–27)," in *On the Bible*, 32.

ways. But the central symbol of all these diverse experiences of the event of liberation became, and remained, the Exodus.[6] The Jews generally could identify with this story as describing what was essential in their experience of being freed by the God of their faith from those who oppressed them.

The Book of Exodus—or at least certain of its strata—clearly goes back to an earlier stage in Israel's history than the Creation stories in Genesis.[7] The liberation from Egypt, placed by scholars in the thirteenth century BC, would have been a necessary precondition for the formation of a people and a history of Israel in the first place. As the founding event of this holy nation, the Exodus would have been necessary first to constitute Israel as a people with a distinctive consciousness of itself, specifically with an identity pivoting on its singularly privileged relationship with God. The image of God as Creator in Genesis in many ways appears to be a development of the image of God as Liberator in the Exodus. The imagery of "dividing" gives the two a common imaginative and structural basis: the dividing of the Red Sea could easily have served as prototype for the divisions (light from darkness, etc.) by which the God of Genesis creates.

From the point of view of historical anthropology, philosophical reflection about origins (in the form of myth) usually comes only after communal life and a cultic matrix have been established and have evolved to a considerable level of sophistication. Only at this stage do the speculative questions that are probed in Genesis come into their own. The origins of the cosmos and the philosophical issues of humanity's place and relations within it would in all likelihood have been treated somewhat later than the historical origins of the people and the effective constituting of the nation. From this perspective, Exodus—even more than Genesis—comes "in the beginning" of the story of the Hebrew people and their religion.

The Hebrew people constantly returned to and meditated on the Exodus as their founding event in order to reaffirm their identity in the present and as directed toward the future. The national self-image forged by the Exodus was in this manner reinterpreted in correspondence with each new situation and its present exigencies in every successive epoch of Hebrew history. Religious truth—specifically the experience of being saved by God—cannot be only an historical fact pertaining to the past: it must

6. Exodus is discussed as "paradigmatic" history by Eric Voegelin, *Israel and Revelation*; and Walter Brueggemann, *An Introduction to the Old Testament: The Canon and Christian Imagination* builds on a similar idea.

7. Von Rad, *Theologie des Alten Testaments*, "Die Anfänge," 17–21, and "Die Herausführung aus Ägypten," 24–26, opens this historical perspective.

also be lived in the present. The narrative of the Exodus sets this event of salvation up as a norm for the present and derives laws from it. Moreover, the Exodus celebrates this event in ritual and liturgical forms, thereby preserving it as an active inspiration and living ideal. All the rememorative reflections upon the Exodus event, including its ritual repetition in liturgical celebration in subsequent times, are to this extent concretely a continuation of the event.

Exodus is an especially perspicuous example of a text that exposes its own use of history for purposes of a people's self-affirmation through ritualistic commemoration of its birth as a nation. The injunction to such liturgical repetition is written into the narrative of the event itself: "And this day shall be unto you for a memorial; and ye shall keep it a feast to the Lord throughout your generations; ye shall keep it a feast by an ordinance for ever" (12:14). The text is constantly concerned with re-actualizing the event it recounts in the present and even in the future: the people addressed in it are not only the original witnesses or hearers in the desert, but also future generations: "your children's children."

Thus the book is expressly attentive not just to the event it relates but also to the process of memorializing it through which history is lived and continually *re*-lived: "And it shall be when thy son asketh thee in time to come, saying, What is this? that thou shalt say unto him, By strength of hand the Lord brought us out from Egypt, from the house of bondage" (13:14). Hence also the reiterated injunctions to remember that are interpolated directly into the midst of the event as narrated: "And Moses said unto the people, Remember this day, in which ye came out from Egypt, out of the house of bondage" (13:3).

With reference to Passover rites, such as sprinkling blood with a branch of hyssop upon lintels and doorposts so that the Lord will "pass over" their houses and strike down only the Egyptians, the text enjoins, "You shall observe this rite as a perpetual ordinance for you and your children. . . . And when your children ask you, 'What do you mean by this observance?' you shall say, 'It is the Passover sacrifice to the Lord, for he passed over the houses of the Israelites in Egypt, when he struck down the Egyptians but spared our houses'" (12:24–27). The Book of Exodus in this way explicitly anticipates its own "Wirkungsgeschichte," literally "history of effect," with its retrospective illumination: history is told for the purpose of embodying a significance of vital importance for the present and for the future times in which it is going to be recited and re-actualized.

II. Discerning the Original Event

The description of the "original" event in Exodus is, in fact, at many points, transparent to innumerable subsequent events of re-actualization in the form of cultic commemoration. The theophany on Mount Sinai, as described in Exodus 19–24, in which the Ten Commandments are given (20:2–17), followed by the Covenant Code (20:22–23; 33), reads for the most part as a description of the ceremony of renewal of the covenant that was performed periodically by the Hebrews in ensuing centuries. Such a ceremony at Schechem, for example, is recorded in Joshua 24 and is reflected in projective remembrance in the closing chapters of Deuteronomy (27–33). Just such acts of ritual repetition in cultic celebration appear to have been superimposed upon the original experience of the Exodus and, in some instances, to have been written right into the account of the Exodus event itself. The meteorological phenomena of cloud and thunder surrounding the sanctuary of the mountain on which the holy event takes place in Exodus 19:16–19 (cf. 20:18) become indistinguishable from clouds of incense and trumpet blasts in ritual celebrations restaging the event for later generations. The narrative tends in this way to conflate the original theophany with its liturgical reenactments. As James Plastras indicates: "The Sinai narrative tells the story of Israel going to meet her God, but it is not just the story of the first generation of Israelites. It is the story of Israel in every generation. It was the story of the current generation who, even as they listened to the narrative, felt themselves standing at the foot of Sinai ready to listen to the voice of God in the liturgical celebration: 'Oh, that *today* you would hear his voice' (Ps 95[94]: 7)."[8]

At the heart of the book, the verse sequence known as the Song of Moses manifestly displays this structure of ritualized use of history in the process of commemoration that creates and maintains national identity by renewing it in each successive age. There is constant alternation between verses pertaining to the specific past event, on the one hand, and more general celebrations of the power and goodness of the Lord, on the other.[9] The opening verse declares that the Lord has triumphed gloriously by throwing horse and rider into the sea. The following verses build on this unique event of the past: they extend it towards a larger field of applications in later times and indeed as a lesson for all time. The second verse reads:

8. Plastras, *The God of Exodus*, 21.

9. The first group comprises verses 1, 4–5, 8–10, 12–17; the second verses 2–3, 6–7, 11, 18. Cf. Charpentier, *Pour Lire l'Ancien Testament*, 30.

> The Lord is my strength and my song,
> and he is become my salvation:
> he is my God, and I will prepare him an habitation;
> my father's God, and I will exalt him.

Nothing in these lines has anything to do specifically with Moses, Pharaoh, or crossing the Red Sea. But these verses express something essential about the God revealed in Exodus for all subsequent generations. The succeeding verses of the Song of Moses make reference to the itinerary of the Israelites among the peoples of Edom, Moab, Canaan, and even to their passing into the promised land and to the building there of a temple. All of this took place long after the event of escape by passing through the sea—the event that the Song ostensibly commemorates. In this manner, the crossing of the Red Sea is projected upon Israel's future: her future, seen in this event's light, is already reflected back into the victory Song itself.[10]

The *incipit* of the Song of Moses, in Exodus 15:1—

> I will sing to the Lord, for he hath triumphed gloriously:
> the horse and his rider hath he thrown into the sea

—is to be counted as among the oldest compositions in the whole Bible. It seems very possible that the sequence of verses comprising the song contains, in poetic form, the germ of the narrative that eventually became the full-blown story of the Exodus.[11] There is a hint that the opening verses may very well be older than the rest of the song, since they appear repeated again verbatim a little later in the chapter, but this time labeled as "Miriam's Song" (15:21). This suggests that they may have existed independently and antecedently to the narrative and that they were already known by another name when they came to be integrated into the Song of Moses and therewith into the narrative recounting the crossing of the Red Sea in chapters 14 and 15. They may even have been composed by an eyewitness to the event—only later to become the originating cell of Moses's Song and thereby perhaps of the entire Exodus epic.[12]

Critical analysis of Exodus has enabled scholars to distinguish different layers of tradition in the climactic event of the crossing of the Red Sea.[13]

10. Alter, *The Art of Biblical Narrative*, speaks here of a "telescoping" of history.

11. This commonplace in Exodus scholarship is treated by Plastras, *The God of Exodus*, 166.

12. Cf. Buber, *Moses: The Revelation and the Covenant*, 74.

13. In addition to Charpentier, *Pour Lire l'Ancien Testament*, 33, see Ska, *Le passage de la mer*, 1–31.

In one account, Jahweh fights side by side with the Israelites; in another he acts only by his word. The first is attributed to the oldest strand of the narrative traditions woven together in Exodus, the J document, in which God is called "Jahweh."[14] It is sometimes dated to the tenth century in Jerusalem under the united monarchy. It represents God anthropomorphically as performing such acts as looking down from the pillar of fire and cloud on the Egyptian army so as to throw it into panic by clogging the wheels of its chariots (14:24–25). This is the God that, like a potter, formed man from the dust of the ground in Genesis 2.

The second account is assigned to the P document elaborated by priestly writers in exile in Babylon during the sixth century BC. This is the source of the priestly theology that left such a clear stamp on Genesis 1, in which God creates by his Word. In the J version, the Lord fights for Israel like a warrior, having driven the sea back by a strong east wind (14:14; 14:21). In the P version, the waters divide under Moses's arm stretched out in a priestly gesture at God's command (14:16). The saying-doing sequence (14:4, 8) and the saving act construed as a "dividing," separating, and making holy are exactly homologous to the creative act in the priestly version of the Creation in Genesis 1. Both idioms for describing the event may appear spliced together in a verse like 14: 21: "Then Moses stretched out his hand over the sea [Priestly]. The Lord drove the sea back by a strong east wind all night, and turned the sea into dry land [Yahwist]; and the waters were divided [Priestly]."

We can never objectively know what actually happened in the Exodus event—and not only because of its being in a remote past, but also because of the nature of religious experience itself as witness rather than objective fact. Nevertheless, we can read and interpret the significance that was attributed to the Exodus in later epochs. And whether we take the J version or the P version, the meaning is that God is revealed as the Liberator of his people. It is the soul of a people—as constituted by their historical memory—that finds expression in this event. Either set of "facts" serves to illustrate the fundamental event, which is a passage not just from one side of the Red Sea to the other, but from fear to freedom. The manifest miracle

14. The very idea of a pre-exilic J document has been effectively questioned since F. V. Winnett, *The Mosaic Tradition.* Since the 1970s, it has been abandoned by many scholars, as we noted in the previous chapter, note 5. Nevertheless, much higher biblical criticism has been turning back to modified forms of the documentary hypothesis, as is remarked by Renaud, *La théophanie du Sinai,* 7.

is the inner transformation, at least from the perspective of the later reenactments, in which the miracle is never over but occurs ever anew.

This type of miraculous event becomes the model for New Testament miracles, where indeed its logic becomes more explicit and deliberate. For example, the return of sight to the eyes of the two blind men in Matthew 9:27–31 is presented as a confirmation and a sign of the primary miracle that has occurred already within their souls: "When he entered into the house, the blind men came to him; and Jesus said to them, Do you believe that I am able to do this?' They said to him, 'Yes, Lord.' Then he touched their eyes and said, 'According to your faith be it unto you.' And their eyes were opened." Their spiritual blindness has been healed already in the instant in which they believe in Jesus, the light of life, and the recovery of sensible sight only ratifies this healing, sealing it with an outward sign.

The miraculous crossing of the Red Sea leads to the theophany and the giving of the Law on Mount Sinai. God's saving act of dividing the waters is completed by the giving of the Law that divides good from evil. In order to truly become God's special people, and thus to be made different from others, Israel must internally appropriate what has befallen it externally. The difference that makes Israel a "chosen people" must be constituted by its own will as a people. For this purpose, the divine law must be not an imposition restricting freedom so much as a way of living liberty itself. Psalm 119 beautifully articulates this sense of the Law as *itself* Israel's salvation and its ardent love ("O, how I love thy law!" v. 97) rather than only an arduous discipline necessary for meriting a reward.

The freedom of the people is expressed par excellence in the history that it remembers and chooses to tell about itself. Genuinely historical significance belongs to the sphere of freedom, not just of fact. In this sense, every aspect of the Exodus epic tells us something about the national identity of the people that adheres to and lives from this account of its origins. It is clear, for example, that the stories of Moses's birth and youth are meant to show how he, as the protagonist of the Exodus epic, was providentially favored in order to relieve his people's oppression. His being saved by "coincidence" in the ark of bulrushes—suggestively echoing Noah's ark—by Pharaoh's daughter hints that God has chosen Moses to lead his people to safety from the Egyptian menace: we discern providence in what appears to be chance. His very name, *Mosheh*, with its reference to his having been "drawn out [Hebrew *mashah*] of the water," as Exodus 2:10 explains, points forward to the Red Sea crossing that draws a whole people out of the watery chaos to salvation, as well as pointing backward to the Flood as a preceding event in which God's salvation was made manifest to Noah.

In each case, allusion is made to God's providential saving of his chosen people. Moses is portrayed as defending the weak against injustice—the Hebrew against the Egyptian, or Jethro's daughters against the shepherds at the well. In different ways, all the elements of the story set him up for his role as defender of his people and representative of God. Not wholly unrelated is his encounter with the burning bush that is not consumed (3:2). This symbol seems to be saying that God is eternal and yet also intensely present in time; holy and mysterious, potentially violent, yet preserving even in his violence.[15] Something like this seems to be symbolized also by the rainbow that follows upon the Flood. But at the center of all these motifs and manifestations, God's paternal care and saving action on behalf of his chosen people is demonstrated in the event that reveals and interprets the meaning of them all—the Exodus.

What I am proposing is that Exodus as a whole be read not as if it were, in some crude form, a documentary history of a unique event in the past but rather as a witness to the Hebrew people's faith across the ages. As such, it represents not objective but relational knowing. A people's sense of being and living in relation to God in all the vicissitudes of its history, its conviction of being cared for and guided, is expressed in the form of epic narrative growing up around its most significant and obsessive memory traces. These crystallizations of memory then engender further expressions in narrative and in lyric traditions.

It is patent that the narrative and even the laws laid down in the Book of Exodus reflect historical conditions pertaining to the time(s) of the book's writing at least as much as to the supposed time of the Exodus event itself. In defining the essential norms for national life, the exigencies of later periods are just as relevant as those proper to the time in which the story is set. The laws recorded in the Book of Exodus actually reflect a number of different phases of society based, for example, on successive nomadic and agricultural economies. By its heterogeneous and "geologically" stratified nature, the Book of Exodus exposes the way in which its own task is not just to record facts, but rather to interpret a sense of national identity as founded upon the relationship with a God who is active as liberator in history, yet also in the present. This liberation is something that must be experienced ever anew by every successive generation.

15. Buber, "The Burning Bush (Exodus 3)," in *On the Bible*.

III. Ongoing Interpretive Re-Actualization

The text of Exodus eminently exemplifies and highlights how epic narrative does not merely recount an event in the historical past but rather displays the process of memory at work in preserving the event and its founding significance by enabling new meaning to accrue to its various features on the basis of lived realities as they are encountered in ensuing epochs. Critical-historical analysis reveals that many of the age-old, traditional feasts of the Hebrew calendar year were given new meaning by being attached to the Exodus event. Certain feasts were quite generally part of the culture of the ancient Near East in which the Hebrews resided. In particular, nomadic peoples of the Near East practiced the sacrifice of a lamb, with spraying of blood on lintels or tents, in order to ward off evil spirits. This custom receives historically specific meaning in the Exodus narrative as a sign for the Angel of the Lord to "pass over" those houses, when smiting the first-born in the land of the Egyptians.

Or again, farmers in the spring, as part of a fertility rite, would celebrate the feast of unleavened bread, discarding old yeast before taking in a new harvest. Exodus's prescriptions for unleavened bread read very cogently as a re-interpretation of such ritual practices in coordination no longer with the cycle of nature but with an historical event. In the context of the Exodus, the readiness to escape in a hurry from Pharaoh's impending pursuit is adduced as the original motivation for this practice that is then ritually repeated in remembrance. Take, for instance, a verse like: "And they baked unleavened cakes of the dough which they brought forth out of Egypt, for it was not leavened; because they were thrust out of Egypt, and could not tarry, neither had they prepared for themselves any victual" (12:39). This has all the appearances of an after-the-fact etiological gloss on a well-established ritual practice.[16]

Such passages interpreting the reasons for ritual practices as connected with the Exodus event strongly suggest that the exigency of memorializing and keeping alive its religious meaning in the present reacted upon the account of the "original" event. The Decalogue itself, which supposedly was given word for word to Moses and inscribed in stone on Mount Sinai, shows signs of having been subjected to interpretation resulting in interpolations in subsequent ages. Formally, the commandments can be broken down into

16. See also 12:26 and 13:14. A number of such presumable adaptations of festival traditions are pointed out by the notes to the Oxford Annotated Bible. Jeffrey J. Niehaus, *Ancient Near Eastern Themes in Biblical Theology* further illuminates such appropriations.

concise prescriptions plus explanatory glosses. For example, the last of the commandments dealing with duties to God enjoins simply, "Remember the Sabbath day, and keep it holy" (20:8). But the following explanation—"For in six days the Lord made heaven and earth, the sea, and all that is in them, and rested the seventh day; therefore the Lord blessed the Sabbath day and hallowed it" (20:11)—evidently depends on the Priestly account of Creation in Genesis 1, which is presumably much later. Surely the practice of the Sabbath antedates this justification given for it.

The whole Pentateuch consists in reinterpretation of traditions—legal, covenantal, ritual, and cultic—in narrative terms and with reference to the all–embracing frame of a national salvation history based on the Exodus. The cultic prescriptions in Exodus 25–31 and 35–40, which are supplemented by the laws of the Holiness Codes in Leviticus 17–26, are given not only for a nomadic people in constant migration, such as the Hebrews were after fleeing from Egypt and while wandering in the desert. Although this is where the giving of these prescriptions is set narratively, they are clearly adapted also to later periods in Israel's history. They deal with the fruit of the harvest and with slaves and much else reflecting more mature stages in the development of Hebrew civilization. Still, all this variety of legislation is shaped by the guiding concept of Israel as a holy people, separated unto the Lord. And Israel first defined and constituted itself as such a people through the Exodus event. Similarly, the account, in the Book of Numbers, of the forty-year sojourn in the wilderness of Sinai reflects the life and crises of the monarchy, the exile in Babylon, and even later periods, all within the narrative framework of the aftermath of the Exodus.

This process continues in the book of Deuteronomy, which means "second law," following upon the law first purportedly given through Moses after the Exodus. Deuteronomy does not only reiterate the Decalogue and Covenant Code: it also thoroughly reinterprets these and other traditions in an effort to recover an acute sense of a special vocation for the Israelite nation. Deuteronomy *preaches* the laws. It is, moreover, cast as Moses's farewell address. Moses is presented no longer as high priest but as prophet, reflecting a shift in the spiritual leadership of Israel and a need to go deeper than mere ritual repetition and achieve a revolutionary renewal of the inspired Word. Deuteronomy proposes a direct experience of God's saving acts in the proclamations of prophecy. This book also advocates reform of worship by means of the centralization of the cult. On the whole, it represents a return to Mosaic traditions, with a zeal to revive their original theological meaning in order to reform and restore Israel morally and religiously, while at the same time adapting these traditions to the very different requirements of an evolving society.[17]

The process of ritual reinterpretation is evident already in the oldest strands of Old Testament tradition, for example, in the primitive Hebrew creed of Deuteronomy 26:5–10: "A Syrian ready to perish was my father, and he went down into Egypt, and sojourned there with a few, and became there a nation, great, mighty, and populous . . ." (cf. 4:32ff). This creedal statement links the offering of first fruits with the Jewish Passover ritual built around the commemoration of the Exodus event: "and the Lord brought us out of Egypt with a mighty hand and an outstretched arm. . . . And now, behold, I have brought the first fruits of the land, which thou, O Lord, hast given me" (26:7–10).

Israel based its faith on historical events—especially on the event of the Exodus as the founding event of its national history. History as a genre is the means through which a people construct their heritage so as to establish their sense of identity as distinct from other peoples. This beginning of historical, revealed religion separates Israel from other ancient peoples and their religions, and it is a momentous novelty in the history of world religions. But it is not hatched full-grown and armed like Athena from Zeus's head. It results, instead, from a long period of incubation. Feeling oneself to be specially chosen is particularly necessary to an infantile understanding of love. Later, the same love can be more maturely recognized as universal in its intrinsic nature. In this manner, the religion of the "chosen people" evolves toward the realization, particularly with the prophets, that God intends to save not only the Jews but all humanity.

The Book of Exodus, as read down through the ages, remains open to a dimension of continuing experience of "exodus" in myriad forms by all peoples. The process of liturgical reenactment and re-actualization has, in fact, extended the founding event far beyond its original matrix and even beyond the boundaries of Hebrew culture. Particularly the Christian religion and specifically the Christ event, especially as celebrated in the Easter liturgy, are themselves founded on the commemoration of the Exodus. Christ, the paschal sacrifice, the sacrifice that saves, is figured as the Passover lamb instituted by the Exodus. In Christian reinterpretation,

17. Deuteronomy's pivotal role in the memnotechnics of the Bible is highlighted by Jan Assmann, *Das kulturelle Gedächtnis*, translated as *Cultural Memory and Early Civilization*.

this sacrifice is linked not just with escape from bondage in Egypt but more universally with liberation from the slavery of sin. Hence Paul sees the Exodus as prefiguring salvation in Christ: he interprets the passage through the sea as a figure for baptism—the sacrament that cleanses Christians from sin by immersion in water and the Spirit. He explicitly states that these things happened to Israel in the Exodus in order to serve as examples or "types" "for us": they are written down for our instruction or "admonition" (1 Cor 10:1–11).

Accordingly, in medieval exegesis, the Exodus becomes the paradigm text for illustrating the four-fold senses of Scripture. Beyond the *literal* sense of the narrative, which recounted the actual historical event of Moses leading the Israelites out of Egypt, the Exodus was understood allegorically in three further, "spiritual" senses. According to its *typological* sense, it was the type or prefiguration of Christ's freeing of the human race from the power of its enemy, Satan. In its *moral* sense, the Exodus represented the escape of the individual human being from the bondage of sin. And, according to its *anagogical* sense, the Exodus signified the delivery of the soul out of this world of time into eternity.[18] These are ways in which the Exodus story opens into an ongoing event of Redemption experienced under various guises by later generations and even in other religions.

If, then, epic history concerns the founding event of a people with a distinct identity and historical destiny, we can return to the question of what history is in the particularly revealing form in which we find it realized in the Book of Exodus. For this book, especially when analyzed into its various layerings of tradition, shows with exemplary clarity how history consists essentially in the interpretation of the past as a means of understanding the present—and with a view to envisaging the future. No history is simply a neutral account of what happened long ago. Every history is written in a historical context of its own that determines inescapably what can be considered to be true and important—or even just intelligible—in the present. History concerns contingent happenings, such as a certain journey from Egypt to Israel, rather than necessary and universal structures of existence, like human creatureliness and ontological dependence. Such universal conditions are apt rather to be represented symbolically as myth. But, like myth, and indeed like every form of literature and of human

18. This technique of the four-fold exegesis of Scripture, as it developed in the Middle Ages, is analyzed in detail by Henri de Lubac, *L'éxégèse médiévale*, translated as *Medieval Exegesis*.

knowledge generally, history treats what is not only an object but involves also a human subject.

Revealing of this subject-object hybridity is the fact that we use the word "history" in two senses. "History" in the sense of what actually happened is the object of "history" or historiography in the sense of the recounting and reconstruction of the past. But, in reality, the two inter-penetrate and are inseparable from each other. For history is nothing if not a dialogue or interaction between events and their recounting. History consists, fundamentally, not in the bald facts of what happened but in the living significance of events as they are remembered and retold. This meaning in the present for those who remember or, more exactly, memorialize events is thrown into vivid relief by humanities texts in general, but it features exemplarily and explicitly in the Book of Exodus. This holy book of Hebrew Scripture leads us near to the "original" sources of biblical tradition in memory and imagination.[19]

19. Walter Benjamin's writings concerning memory and history, signally *Berliner Chronik, Einbahnstraße*, and "On the Concept of History" ("Über den Begriff der Ge-schichte" 1940) included in *Angelus Novus*, theoretically illuminate the legacy of this especially Jewish sensibility for living memory, which continues to unfold down to our own times.

CHAPTER 4

The Prophetic Voice: Inspired Interpretation of Historical Destiny

I. Prophecy and the Genres of Revelation

WE HAVE SEEN SO far that revelation, whether of fundamental conditions of human existence (myth) or of the founding event of a nation (epic history), cannot abstract from the present moment and the particular situation of those for whom it occurs. Revelation occurs for them, moreover, specifically in and through their own acts of interpretation. To this extent, revelation of a mythic or of an historical past is always also *self-*revelation in which latter-day interpreters find their own reality mirrored and disclosed in the past as refracted by the newly-breaking light of actual experience. Revelation inevitably involves this dimension of the interpreters' lived experience, in which the *event* of revelation occurs—or rather *re*curs—in the present.

Prophecy, the next genre to which we turn, continues and intensifies the process of actualizing or contemporizing revelation in present acts of interpretation that mythic and historical imagination in their different ways already embody and exemplify. Cast in the generic mold of prophecy, divine revelation is formulated as the present utterance of God in person. Since revelation in the biblical sense can only be realized in the present tense of a living relationship with God, myth and history are finally fulfilled in their revelatory meaning as purportedly "divine" disclosure of human life only in prophecy, which speaks as if directly from God's own point of view and even in God's own voice.

The whole Bible is "prophetic" in the sense that it is all divine revelation, all "the Word of God." However, the narrower sense of "prophecy," as a distinct genre among others in the Bible, turns upon a specifically prophetic rhetoric that makes fully explicit in its form of enunciation the hypothesis that God is speaking and that he is personally addressing his people. In narrative genres, such as the Creation myth and the Exodus epic, this first-person address of God to humans remains almost entirely implicit. But the oracular form used in prophecy formally reports God's own speech directly. This is often indicated explicitly by phrases such as "Thus saith the Lord" or "Hear ye the word of the Lord." For example, the beginning of the Book of Isaiah first announces that the Lord has spoken and then moves into an actual address from the Lord God as "I":

> Hear, O heavens, and give ear, O earth:
> for the Lord hath spoken,
> *I* have nourished and brought up children,
> and they have rebelled against me. (Isa 1:2)

This opening welds a reprise of Genesis 1:1 ("In the beginning, God created the heavens and the earth") together with a direct address from God, who speaks in the first person as "I." It also alludes to the history of God's relationship with his people and to their rebelliousness, which is often recalled also in Exodus, for example, in the incident of the golden calf (Exodus 32).

Pro-phecy (from the Greek φάσις–assertion, via the Latin *fateor*–confession) means "speaking out" and, in effect, is a speaking *for* ("pro") God. Hence the broad sense in which the whole of the Bible, as the "Word of God," is prophetic. But the books that are labeled "prophetic" in the stricter sense of the word render this fact explicit: they attempt to dramatically realize the divine voice. The vocative is the fundamental mode of prophetic address. It is nominally God in the first person who directly addresses his people in prophetic discourse. The statements that result are very aptly called "oracles."

In content, prophecy is about (re)interpreting for the present the meaning of revelation as it has been crystallized in tradition. Thus a vital task of the prophets was to revive in their contemporary relevance certain hoary religious traditions, such as those of Creation and Exodus, that for some had grown cold and become *mere* history and empty ritual. The prophets aimed to bring back—in all its urgency for the present, with its decisions and dilemmas—the demand of God for obedience especially to justice and therewith for reform and repentance. This phenomenon of returning to and revitalizing religious traditions can be documented within the Bible preeminently in relation to the Exodus narration. A great deal of prophetic influence is channeled into Deuteronomy, the "second law," in which the original Mosaic Law from Exodus is re-proposed, but as adapted to new historical conditions and as ardently preached.[1] Not mere exterior actions of ceremony and cultic sacrifice, but a heart sincerely moved in its depths and turned (literally "con-verted") to God was demanded by the prophets.

The basis for the prophet's interpretation of history, including contemporary history, is a personal relationship with God. This is established for Isaiah in the account of his vocation or calling. Chapter 6 dramatically describes Isaiah's vision of the King, the Lord of hosts, seated on his throne on high and surrounded by ministering and worshipping seraphim. It culminates in the sending of the prophet on his mission, after his lips have been touched with a live coal and thus purified. This, in effect, authorizes the prophet to interpret history as if from the divine point of view. This was implicitly the case in Exodus, too: Moses is its "author," and his authority is based on his being the prophet who functions as mediator in Israel's relationship with God at that crucial juncture in its history. But now a formal change comes about. In prophecy, God himself is speaking. The "pro-phet" is one in whom God directly speaks, and this makes for the formal difference between the prophetic and the "historical" books, which nevertheless are tellingly subsumed as the "former prophets," suggesting the broader sense in which they, too, are prophetic, albeit less explicitly so, since they lack the form of direct first-person address from the Almighty.

The books that are properly prophetic in the strict sense by virtue of their rhetorical form as oracles in which God directly speaks take on also—and not by accident—a more pronounced poetical character. Prophecy addresses specific historical agents and situations, yet its poetic form also generalizes its messages beyond their original contexts. This has been shown effectively in relation to Isaiah 1 in a detailed reading by Robert

---

1. Von Rad's studies of Deuteronomy in *Old Testament Theology: The Theology of Israel's Historical Traditions* are pioneering in this regard.

Alter.[2] Our main purpose in what follows is to explore the implications of the *poetic form* of prophecy as exemplified chiefly by this prophet.

As we move into the genre of prophecy in biblical literature, the interpretation of the historical past or of mythic origins in terms of present experience and its significance is not left behind: it becomes even more urgent. It comes out into the open at this point that myth and history from the beginning of the Bible have been implicitly a kind of prophecy. Prophecy presents, once again, the Creator God, "who has measured the waters in the hollow of his hand / and marked off the heavens with a span" (Isaiah 40:12), as well as the Lord of history, "who brings princes to naught, / and makes the rulers of the earth as nothing" (40:23). Prophecy recapitulates these mythological and historical motifs from the Genesis and the Exodus traditions, but it attempts to reinterpret them as relevant to and prescriptive for a contemporary context. Each new present predicament needs to be dealt with through recollection of these traditions, and the prophets make this exigency programmatic. In prophecy, furthermore, history and myth are clearly revealed as human mediations of divine revelation, such as the Bible as a whole represents. Interpretation of history, no less than the interpretation of fundamental conditions of human existence, can be determined not as matters of objective fact but only in a dimension of freedom, of free response to the call of God that the prophet makes to be heard again, beseeching and pleading for genuine faith in the God who has revealed himself in history and creation.

Thus prophecy incorporates and redeploys the sorts of historical and mythic discourses that we have already considered, but in prophecy the present horizon of significance—which we have already stressed as covertly decisive for all interpretation, whether historical or mythic or symbolic—is brought directly into view. Present threats of destruction and promises of deliverance are overtly the prophet's theme. He aims expressly to act within and impinge upon the present predicament of the nation. He is not just saying what will inevitably happen—any more than the biblical historian is saying merely what, as a matter of fact, took place. He is provoking an examination of conscience and is attempting to influence behavior by bringing about a certain self-understanding in which his audience will recognize itself as God's chosen people. In this way, prophecy is an even more highly evolved and explicit example than we have had so far of how humanities

2. Alter, *The Art of Biblical Poetry*, 142ff.

texts reinterpret tradition so as to realize its truth in the crucible of the present—and thereby also in a fashion that is exemplary for all ages.

II. Oracular Form and Poetic Power in Isaiah

Prophecy formally is the speech of God cast into oracles announced by the prophet, who serves as spokesperson or mouthpiece. A model for this relationship is the way Aaron served as "mouth" for Moses, who was "as God" to him (Exod 4:14–16). Accordingly, prophecy is distinguished first by its vocative character. It is addressed to Israel, and to other human agents, as audience. It modulates from invective to accusation and satire; it employs sarcasm and name-calling, as well as the more positive modes of comforting, praising, and promising. But in all of these moods, the poetic form of these utterances serves also to maintain a high degree of indeterminacy for what God says.[3] It is especially this poetic character of prophetic oracles that makes them fit to communicate *God's* message and gives them universal scope and meaning.

The "oracles" in which prophecy principally consists typically speak to specific historical situations and agents. They address, for example, a city with an invader approaching: the people is accused of apostasy or corruption and is enjoined to understand the immanent catastrophe as a condign punishment for its sins. By such means, prophecies make a powerful argument and urgent appeal for immediate reform. Prophecies are not general maxims or logical reflections but spontaneous eruptions of difficult truth—disclosures of God and of his demands for justice in concrete crises. However, they also have a tendency to exceed the requirements of their immediate historical situations. They are not just recipes for practical reform. Particularly their poetic form promotes prophetic oracles to messages of much more general purport and far–reaching significance: they become religiously valid revelations of the eternal fidelity of God and of the ways of his providential involvement in history. Transfigured into poetry, the historically specific messages of prophecy take on paradigmatic significance for human societies and individuals. In Isaiah 14, for example, the prophecy against the king of Babylon is elaborated with such imaginative amplitude and power as to transform its subject into an archetype of evil.

3. Brueggemann, *Theology of the Old Testament* also pertinently emphasizes that prophets "speak most often with all the elusiveness and imaginative power of poetry" (625). He develops this insight in his *The Prophetic Imagination*.

From "How hath the oppressor ceased! the golden city ceased!" this passage modulates into a cosmological register, evoking forces of good and evil in the universe[4]:

> How art thou fallen from heaven, O Lucifer, son of the morning!
> how art thou cut down to the ground, which didst weaken the nations!
> For thou hast said in thine heart, I will ascend into heaven,
> I will exalt my throne above the stars of God:
> I will sit also upon the mount of the congregation,
> in the sides of the north;
> I will ascend above the heights of the clouds;
> I will be like the most High. (Isa 14:12–14)

Similarly ranging from the specific to the symbolic, the "servant of the Lord" in Isaiah can sometimes be identified with the historical king of the Persians, Cyrus, who is called by name, for example, in 44:28 and 45:1. Cyrus served the Lord in bringing about the fall of the Babylonian Empire in 539 BC, thereby freeing subject peoples like Israel to return home out of exile. And yet too narrow and exclusive an identification of such figures in prophecy runs the risk of compromising their manifold resonances in later history. The suffering servant of Isaiah 53 will come to be recognized, for instance, anachronistically, as Christ in his Passion redeeming our sins:

> But he was wounded for our transgressions,
> he was bruised for our iniquities:
> the chastisement of our peace was upon him;
> and with his stripes we are healed. (Isa 53:5)

The poetry of such figures resides not least in their miraculously elastic identity, which enables unexpected connections to be made later in history, as the Crucifixion narratives richly attest, with their manifold allusions to Isaiah.

The form of prophecy itself, by using the specific and concrete to communicate something more ideal and general, is eminently poetic. Such poetic language is necessarily the form required for communicating the Word of God in God's own voice by direct discourse. For such communication

4. Compare the reading of this passage offered by Alter, *The Art of Biblical Poetry*, 146. Deeper in the background here is the stylistic analysis of Isaiah by Hermann Gunkel, generally recognized as the founder of so-called "form-criticism." Pages 34–70 from his *Die Propheten* are translated by James L. Schaaf and excerpted in Petersen, *Prophecy in Israel*, 22–73.

entails expression of what in principle transcends all determinate objects and all literal expression in language. How could God speak in any one finite voice except provisionally and poetically? Poetry achieves an indeterminacy of language that opens upon infinity. This does not exclude precision and concreteness: on the contrary, these qualities are necessary, and in any case highly conducive, to poetic expression. Still, all determinate, literal meaning in poetry is but a gesture beyond itself towards a meaning that is metaphorical, or open and infinite. Literal meaning is not denied but is transfigured into another, an unbounded register of significance.

It is not easy to say what poetry is, but one good way to experience it in certain of its peculiarly formidable powers is simply to read the book of Isaiah aloud in the King James Version. The sublimity of the conception of God, who remains, of course, undefined and out of sight, is expressed in the measureless intensity of the language that flows from the unattainable height of his sovereignty. Such language asserts the Lord's authority over life and death and affirms his visceral passion for his people. The prophet's poetic afflatus makes for breath-taking strophes such as:

> All flesh is grass,
> and all the goodliness thereof is as the flower of the field:
> The grass withereth, the flower fadeth:
> because the spirit of the Lord bloweth upon it:
> surely the people is grass.
> The grass withereth, the flower fadeth:
> but the word of our God shall stand for ever. (Isa 40:6–7)

It may be necessary to read several chapters consecutively before, by its cumulative effect, the poetry builds to its full momentum and succeeds in conveying unshakeable conviction. A steady concentration is required in order to feel oneself swept up by the rapid clip of the verses in their rhythmic swelling to sublime intimations that communicate not concepts so much as a cloudy sense of an overwhelming presence. This poetry evokes fear and awe by exposing the littleness of all that is human and worldly as compared with the greatness of God that rings through lines like those describing the Day of Judgment:

> Enter ye into the rock,
> and hide thee in the dust,
> for fear of the Lord, and for the glory of his majesty.
> The lofty looks of man shall be humbled,

and the haughtiness of men shall be bowed down,
and the Lord alone shall be exalted in that day. (Isa 2:10–11)

The language is lofty and exalted, yet at the same time unaffected and humble, highly styled and yet startlingly immediate, using whatever homely metaphors may be ready to hand: "the ox knoweth his owner, the ass his master's crib"; "a heritage for hedgehogs"; "And the daughter of Zion is left as a cottage in a vineyard, as a lodge in a garden of cucumbers . . . ." Such language retains its jagged edges, as the imagery itself insists: "To go into the clefts of the rocks, and into the tops of the ragged rocks." For all its classical poise and rhetorical polish, the style manages to remain remarkably abrupt and rough. Sudden epiphanies of recognition tend to interrupt any effort at methodical development.

Crude images of unrefinement and wildness only add to the raw power and intensity of such poetic diction, which describes princely palaces abandoned to moles and bats, to briers and thorns, to wild asses. A small handful of recurrent motifs—chastisement, forgiveness, restoration, exaltation, and rejoicing—make up the repertoire of these poems and are made to pass through imponderable intensities of emotion. It does not necessarily matter at first exactly what is being denounced or exulted over: the degree of affect alone is a revelation in its own right. At the emotional height from which such conceits spring forth, they seem inevitable, however fanciful and far-fetched:

It is he that sitteth upon the circle of the earth,
and the inhabitants thereof are as grasshoppers;
that stretcheth out the heavens as a curtain,
and spreadeth them out as a tent to dwell in.

(Isa 40:22)

Exactly appropriate, pungent images make for memorable phrases that become proverbial, such as the "drop in the bucket" and "small dust in the balance" (40:15), the heavens "rolled together as a scroll" (34:4), or "they shall beat their swords into plowshares, and their spears into pruninghooks" (2:4). Every image flashes out with the rapidity of lightning. The imagination makes always an immediate leap to the concrete. No coldly calculated analyses of moral corruption in Israel but rather excruciatingly detailed description of a horridly diseased body:

The whole head is sick, and the whole heart faint.
From the sole of the foot even unto the head
there is no soundness in it;
But wounds, and bruises, and putrifying sores:
They have not been closed, neither bound up, neither mollified
    with ointment. (Isa 1:5–6)

The dimension of poetry is essential to humanities texts in general, given their relative freedom from the matrices in which they originate and their susceptibility to being reappropriated ever again in new circumstances and different contexts. Aristotle noted that poetry possesses the universality of truth that is lacking to history (*Poetics*, chapter 7). And this is why poetry is essentially the medium of tradition—that is, of truth that must be found over and over again by succeeding generations and so establishes its universality. In this manner, the fundamental indeterminacy of meaning in poetic language becomes instrumental to the inexhaustible life of the traditional text.

III. The Raptures of Isaiah: Their Influence Down to Jesus and Beyond

The Book of Isaiah particularly illustrates how revelation is achieved in and through poetic language. Universalization of meaning can be achieved when historically specific oracles directed towards designated agents in given historical settings are cast into poetic form. This is especially evident in Isaiah's prophecies and is part of the reason why Isaiah has lent itself so well to Christian appropriations. Indeed, the drive toward the universalization of revelation lies at the heart of this book, even at a thematic level. The theme of opening faith in Israel's God to all peoples is, perhaps more than anything else, what makes it one book. Compiled together under the name "Isaiah" in our Bibles are the works of at least three distinguishable prophets: pre-exilic (second half of the eighth century BC), exilic (just before 539 BC), and post-exilic (530–510 BC).[5] But the universal opening of revelation and salvation to the Gentiles is ecstatically announced already in "First

---

5. This picture has been made even more complex through the theories of growth by accretion, according to which the prophetic books are perhaps accumulations of writings attached to the name of the original prophet who founded what was at first only an oral tradition. See Jacques Vermeylen, *Du prophète Isaïe à l'apocalyptique: Isaïe, I–XXXV*, 2 vols.; and Luis Alonso Schökel, "Isaiah," in *The Literary Guide to the Bible*.

Isaiah," which comprises basically chapters 1–39, from the second chapter of the book: "And it shall come to pass in the last days, that the mountain of the Lord's house shall be established in the top of the mountains, and shall be exalted above the hills; and all nations shall flow unto it . . ." (2:25).

A universal redemption not only of history but also of nature is envisaged in the prospect of a return to Edenic peace and amity among all creatures:

> The wolf also shall dwell with the lamb
> and the leopard shall lie down with the kid . . . .
> They shall not hurt nor destroy
> in all my holy mountain:
> for the earth shall be full of the knowledge of the Lord,
> as the waters cover the sea. (Isa 11:6–9)

In "Third Isaiah," the note of universality is again struck in the triumphant chapters 60–63, beginning "Arise, shine; for your light has come, and the glory of the Lord has risen upon you. . . . Nations shall come to your light, and kings to the brightness of your dawn." But the generalization of revelation through poetic universality is realized perhaps most convincingly of all by Second Isaiah (chapters 40–55), from whom the phrase "I will also give thee as a light to the Gentiles" (49:6 and 42:6) is borrowed by Luke 2:32 and woven into the Song of Simeon and therewith into the liturgy of the Church. This promise of universal human enlightenment through the Jewish messiah has, in fact, been conserved throughout the centuries in the Roman Catholic monastic liturgy: it is recited at the end of each day at the office of compline, the last of the seven canonical hours.

Second Isaiah, moreover, is particularly prized for its unsurpassable expression of sheer exaltation. "Sing, O barren, thou that didst not bear; break forth into singing . . ." (54:1). The emotions are of an intensity that transcends any specific situation and becomes exemplary of sheer unadulterated glorying and exultation. The feelings expressed are not necessarily bound to any single series of events. One requires at first no complex and differentiated understanding of the historical context and causes of these sentiments: in their intensity alone they are immediate, irresistible, and overwhelming.

> Sing, O ye heavens; for the Lord hath done it:
> shout, ye lower parts of the earth:
> break forth into singing, ye mountains,

O forest, and every tree therein:
for the Lord hath redeemed Jacob,
and glorified himself in Israel. (Isa 44:23)

Isaiah is by common consent the lyrical apogee of the prophetic books and therewith of at least a certain type of poetry in the Bible. Perhaps only the Book of Job has been equally praised for the matchless excellence of its poetry. These judgments hold surprisingly well for readings in both Hebrew and in English. The King James Version of the Book of Isaiah ranks among the very highest poetic masterpieces of English literature. But not only does Isaiah, with its rare poetic distinction, come first in the corpus of the prophets (*Nebiim*) in the Hebrew Bible: Isaiah also has a special role in anticipating and announcing the Christian Gospel. It is in Isaiah that we read:

How beautiful upon the mountains
Are the feet of him that bringeth good tidings,
That publisheth peace;
That bringeth good tidings of good,
That publisheth salvation . . . (Isa 52:7ff.)

Isaiah's uncannily evangelical power is graphically illustrated further in *Acts of the Apostles* 8:26–39, where it is by explaining passages from Isaiah that the apostle Philip converts the Ethiopian court eunuch, who leaps down from his chariot to receive baptism immediately.

In the Gospels, Jesus himself has special regard for Isaiah: he reads from this book publicly in the synagogue (Luke 4:16–21). The Gospel writers pick up on a host of its prophecies, centrally the description of the suffering servant (Isa 52:13ff), with whom Jesus in his Passion is identified. Not surprisingly, then, Isaiah also furnishes an abundance of source texts for later liturgical and artistic celebrations of the Gospel story, some very popular, such as Handel's *Messiah*. This prophetic book distinguishes itself by the way it contributes to the realization of tradition—namely, through the perennial reprise of traditional motifs relived in novel contexts and as disclosing truth anew. The book thus bridges between epochs and unifies history. The poetic quality of the text is surely not accidental or irrelevant to this result: it is perhaps principally poetry that enables this process of synthesis by virtue of its polysemousness and the inexhaustible fertility of its meanings. Certainly the deep, humanly moving power of poetry motivates a continual return to verbal traditions for the sake of their reappropriation in new historical predicaments.

Isaiah's lyric rapture is essential, moreover, to revelation as "out of this world." It is by the transports of poetry that a dimension of existence beyond representation—the invisible, unrepresentable divine transcendence—can be intimated. Poetry can give us a fleeting sense of eternity—for instance, in Rimbaud's "L'éternité." Poetry in the Hebrew prophets, as in poets of all ages, runs up against the limit of the inexpressible. But prophecy motivates this formal limit of poetry thematically in terms of its primary subject matter—God. The sublimity of God revealed by Isaiah resides in what is *not* revealed about him. To this extent, Isaiah has no express theology and no articulated idea of God, except that he is incomparably higher than any idea we can possibly have of him: "To whom then will ye liken God? or what likeness will ye compare unto him?" (40:18). The inaccessible height of God's transcendence, which can make him a hidden God, a *Deus absconditus* (45:15), is definitively expressed by Isaiah:

> For my thoughts are not your thoughts,
>> neither are your ways my ways, saith the Lord.
> For as the heavens are higher than the earth,
>> so are my ways higher than your ways,
>> and my thoughts than your thoughts." (Isa 55:8–9)

This gap between our thoughts and God points towards the passage beyond representation altogether: it points toward a total rupture with the world as we know it, and thereby towards "apocalypse."

IV. From Prophecy to Apocalyptic

Prophecy interprets history and existence in the light of revelation. It interprets them explicitly into the present, in which challenges must be faced courageously and decisions must be made, not least about faith. But even while addressing the ever so specific situations of a people undergoing all manner of tribulation, prophecy also delivers messages whose validity is much wider and potentially unbounded. Prophecy speaks out of its particular historical situation to all times with a universal message claiming to reveal the God of history and the cosmos. Prophecy does this especially by virtue of its poetic form.

Prophecy can perhaps best be defined as the poetic interpretation of history in the light of revelation. In a prophetic perspective, history is lived in the present and is the mirror of the future. For the biblical prophets, history is providentially ruled by the one eternal God who acts with one purpose from the beginning of time to the end. In this way, the vulgar meaning of prophecy as foretelling the future can be comprehended within the definition of prophecy as inspired interpretation of history. But *fore*-sight is only one dimension of the *in*sight into history—into its purpose and destiny—that is realized much more completely by prophecy in the deeper sense of the word.

Predicting the future is perhaps the most sensational aspect of prophetic vision. For there seem to be other, natural ways of knowing the past and the present but not the future, since the future has not yet happened, nor been seen. Yet, for Isaiah the prophet, knowing the future is probably not different in kind from knowing the whole dispensation of the divine will from the foundations of the world:

> Have ye not known? have ye not heard?
> hath it not been told you from the beginning?
> have ye not understood from the foundations of the earth?

(Isa 40:21)

The prophets do often project their oracles into the past in order to make them anticipate cataclysmic events. Second Isaiah "predicts" the campaigns of Cyrus the Persian, culminating in the fall of Babylon in 538 BC, when they are already underway. The Book of Daniel was written between 167 and 164 BC, under the persecution of the Hellenistic Seleucid Emperor Antiochus IV Epiphanes that led to the Maccabean revolt in the aftermath of the Greek control of Palestine by the successors of Alexander the Great, who had died in 323 BC. The author—"Daniel"—assumes the name of a *persona* from a much earlier age, the Babylonian captivity in the sixth century BC, in order to project forward, with the sureness of hindsight, already accomplished facts. But this only further confirms that rather than being prediction of the future prophecy is essentially interpretation of history in such a way as to reveal its divine significance, its meaning from the point of view of God.

Only because the past and future are embraced together in the present—God's eternal present—can the prophet "see" the future. Understanding history enables the prophet to discern the essential shape of things to come. It is not by magic, not by command over an otherwise inaccessible field of objects, that the prophet sees the future. He sees it, rather, by identifying with God through grace and inspiration to such an extent that his interpretations themselves become instrumental to the realization of the divine purpose in history. They prophesy the future because they anticipate and participate in it—and indeed even help to bring it about. They situate themselves within the horizon of the revelation of God and his providential plan, making its implications compellingly evident to human beings. This is why prophecy leads inevitably to apocalypse, where the interpretation of history reveals the final sense of history as a whole beyond the limits of history as such. This sense might thus be said to issue out of the womb of eternity, into whose secret depth the vision of apocalypse darkly penetrates.

By virtue of its centrifugal energies, driving toward ever greater scope and significance, prophecy tends to lead to a projection from history into eternity. And this takes it to the threshold of apocalypse. The Book of Isaiah, from its very beginning, is about the imminent judgment of God and "the Day of the Lord": the "last days" are announced (2:2). The sequence commencing "Enter into the rock" (2:10) already imagines the cataclysm of the Lord coming in his majesty, "When he ariseth to shake terribly the earth." But it is particularly chapters 24–27, together with 34–35—known respectively as the great and little Isaiah apocalypses—that have been recognized as constituting veerings into actual apocalyptic.

To an even greater extent, the book of Daniel is distinguished among the prophetic books for modulating from prophecy into apocalyptic. This becomes especially clear and explicit in the final chapters (10–12). An angel-like "man" (10:5) comes to Daniel to make him understand what is to befall his people "in the latter days." This is a vision "for days yet to come" (10:14). In apocalyptic, history is interpreted from the point of view not only of divine revelation but specifically of the revelation of its end. The purpose of the book of Daniel as a whole is significantly different from that of the prophets and is to be understood rather as specifically apocalyptic. Daniel does not directly address his people in order to exhort or reprove and chastise them. He writes to encourage and provide comfort and reassurance in times of dire hardship by promising an imminent intervention on the part of God in defense of his people. A triumphant finale to all their tribulation in the present is discerned as waiting in the wings. This inspires hope that in an already encroaching future, the time of the end will erupt and usher in the advent of eternity.

Apocalyptic is concerned not so much with reform, or with relations within this world. The focus is no longer on God's becoming effectively present in history through the actions of human beings: it shifts to the other world and to God's action to overthrow the historical order as a whole. Exotic allegorical visions adumbrate this transformation. The revelations to Daniel are ones that Daniel himself does not understand (12:8); they are sealed up in a book until the time of the end (12:4). There is no longer the visionary transparency enjoyed by the prophets as interpreters of the divine. This is signified also by the introduction of mediators like the angels Gabriel and Michael. They are an index, as Shemaryahu Talmon explains, of "the unbridgeable chasm which increasingly separates man from the divine sphere. In the biblical past, a prophet could bring God's word to man. Now, the seer requires a celestial interpreter to explain his visions to him. Mediator upon mediator intervenes between man and God. And even then the meaning of the revelation may remain hidden."[6] In the second half of Daniel, that is, in chapters 7–12, after the court stories of chapters 1–6, very late prophetic and now more properly apocalyptic writing tends to narrow the interpretive faculties of the prophet, who becomes more a mechanical mouthpiece for relaying purportedly objective facts about the future.

These apocalyptic visions are mostly concerned, in various guises, with the succession of empires in the ancient world as leading to total corruption and disaster and as issuing finally in the reign of God. After Egypt and Assyria, world empire will pass to Babylon (607 BC), to Medes and Persians (539 BC), to Greece (331 BC), and to Rome (30 BC). This succession is encoded into the series of metals (gold, silver, bronze, iron/earth) composing the sections of the statue in Nebuchadnezzar's dream (Daniel 2). Daniel also elaborates the images of beasts rising with numerous heads from the depths and a speaking horn that will reappear in the Christian apocalypse par excellence, the Revelation of St. John the Divine. There is a whole genre of inter-testamental apocalypses (2 Esdras, 2 Baruch, 1 Enoch, etc.) spouting this sort of inebriating imagery with its surreal scenography.

Yet it is important that apocalyptic not be limited to or centered upon these fantastic visions; neither should the apocalyptic mode be confined to the specific genre that fosters them. The prophets and even the Gospels are themselves already intrinsically apocalyptic, or at least "eschatological," in the sense of envisaging the end (*eschaton*, in Greek). The apocalypses per se as a separate corpus of writings often tend to decline from the exalted poetic vision of the prophetic voice mysteriously refracting the speech of God into a factual rhetoric of revenge detailing inescapable future chastisements. In contrast, the apocalyptic moments *within* prophecy, as it occurs

6. Talmon, "Daniel," in *The Literary Guide to the Bible*, 350.

in both the Old Testament and the New, envision the end in its intrinsic connection with the present and in the tension of the fateful decisions that the present exacts. Rather than attempting to declare in pseudo-factual rhetoric, in the style of the inter-testamental apocalypses, what will unfailingly come to pass, the Gospels and the prophets alike invite to living within a vision of the end that enables humans to work for realizing the highest possibilities of their present. Such apocalyptic and eschatological moments throughout the Bible are open to receiving the revelation of God through the interpretive mediation of humans rather than formalizing it into a fixed code of images and a set repertoire of dramatic disasters. In this way—apocalyptic, too—rather than appearing only as the final unveiling of a supposedly unequivocal, positive truth participates in revelation as it is progressively discovered through the unfolding process of a succession of poetic genres in the Bible.[7]

The idea of apocalyptic revelation is a very challenging one within the framework of human and historical study. It threatens history with annihilation and is therefore often rejected by the historical (when not outright historicist) outlook of a great part of contemporary cultural criticism.[8] But considered in light of the non-objective nature of knowledge in the humanities, apocalyptic belongs essentially to the Western intellectual tradition as a whole—at its limit. It is surely no objective knowledge of events, but nevertheless it seems to be a necessary structure of the striving to come to full knowledge of oneself, since this requires transcending the self and every manifest phenomenon of the world that can be seen.[9]

---

7. I elaborate these theses in theoretical terms in *Poetry and Apocalypse: Theological Disclosures of Poetic Language*, 8–19.

8. Roskies, *Against Apocalypse*.

9. The widely felt human need for apocalyptic access to worlds unseen is confirmed by intriguing comparison, beyond Western traditions, with Mayan, Himalayan, Siberian, and other cultures in John Leavitt, *Poetry and Prophecy: The Anthropology of Inspiration*.

CHAPTER 5

The Writing of Revelation: Witness and Address

I. Human Voice and Self-Expression

WE HAVE NOW SEEN how myth, history, and prophecy can all be used as vehicles of religious revelation. But what of consciously literary art? The prophets, in spite of all their poetic imagery and rhetoric, spoke in God's name and delivered oracles as direct speech in God's own voice. In the Writings, human voices expressing human concerns emerge and present themselves as such: they directly expose the affective and volitional dimensions of human existence. Whereas in the Prophets, in accordance with the formal structure of the oracle, God speaks to humans, in the Writings (*Ketubim* in Hebrew) it is human beings who are speaking to and about God. Perhaps most conspicuously, the Psalms speak for humanity: they speak from and of its hopes and fears. They voice its miseries and triumphs, its sense of comfort or guilt or trust or doubt referred directly to a divinity in relation to whom all human experiences are lived and articulated. Typically these voices are addressed to God, who is praised and revered, feared, pleaded with, thanked, complained to, quarreled with, and queried. The human voices of the Writings, moreover, are of different types of "radical"—the root, or generative source, of discourse in a situated communication. While in the prayer of the Psalms most often an anonymous, universal human voice is speaking, usually in a communal and sometimes also liturgical language, in Ecclesiastes a highly self-conscious

"I" steps forward and identifies himself as a distinct and indeed a very distinguished individual.

With the vector of communication reversed with respect to prophecy, the Writings open in myriad new directions. We have humanity speaking to and about God in a great variety of literary forms, including prayer (Psalms), lament or threnody (Lamentations), philosophical meditations (Ecclesiastes), love lyrics (Song of Songs), drama (Job), and wise sayings (Proverbs). Such diversity of artistic forms is deployed to explore the inexhaustible *human* dimensions and depth of the experience of God. This has, in effect, already been the case, indirectly yet inevitably, in Myth, History, and Prophecy: each genre in its own way is based on human mediation of divine revelation. But now a more self-consciously human and artistic sifting of the meaning of the experience deposited in Israel's traditions is brought into the foreground and elaborated. Without attenuating the claim to deliver a revelation from and of God, the Writings for the first time give us the full sense of humanity expressing itself directly in its own voice and sometimes even in an outspokenly personal way.

Of course, in all that we have read so far, humanity could not help but express itself. Nonetheless, the requirements of the previous genres relegated the expression of human sentiment and sensibility to the margins as epiphenomena. What the experience felt like to the human beings involved was, at least in principle, secondary. The human voice was muted or masked in a variety of ways in the preceding genres: behind the voice of God in prophecy; in favor of the (purported) facts themselves in epic history; in deference to impersonal, universal conditions of existence in myth. In the Writings, the sphere of subjective human experience, on the part both of a people and of individuals, is opened up to being probed and articulated with all the deliberate aesthetic self-consciousness of a highly refined literary art.

How are the experiences of God, history, and the existence of human beings in the world actually lived? What feelings are produced and how can they be expressed? Human subjectivity—individual and collective—opens in the Writings as a further dimension in which revelation is discovered and progressively unfolds. Still, even as overtly human expression, this part of the Bible is equally to be considered God's Word. In the Writings, it becomes fully transparent that human and divine agencies are to be conceived of as collaborating and even as coinciding in the composition of the Bible, which the two are indeed figured as co-authoring. What binds all these human, often all-too-human, modes of expression together is their function as divine revelation. In the Writings, even artistic exploration of the human experience of the world and the psyche in relation to God is presented as inspired by faith and as revelatory of manifold intimate aspects of a personal God. The embrace of such writings as divine revelation and as equal in status to oracles spoken in the voice of the Almighty expresses the intuition that God is present in all of Creation, including human creations. Recognizing the Writings as inspired also expresses the realization that any representation of divinity inevitably participates in a degree of fiction.

II. Existential Crisis in Ecclesiastes

Ecclesiastes (in Hebrew *Qohelet,* meaning "Preacher," "Speaker," or sometimes "Teacher") presents a very personal author with his private palaces, parks, forests, fruit trees, and hundreds of concubines. The strong sense of individuality and even of intimately personal experience, with its usually tacit satisfactions and frustrations, makes Ecclesiastes a book that many readers are apt to feel close to today. Perhaps an even more strikingly modern aspect—and a direct consequence of this high degree of subjective self-consciousness—is that Ecclesiastes expresses doubts about the meaning of life. The sense of life's absurdity, its meaninglessness, its "vanity," resonates with more recent types of thinking like existentialism or the "philosophy of the absurd" that epitomize the modern era. In fact, it has often been debated whether and why this book should have been canonized and included in the Bible at all, since to many it seems more expressive of existential *Angst* and despair than of religious faith. An editor of the Oxford Annotated Bible, for instance, introduces the work with the comment that, "Ecclesiastes contains the reflections of a philosopher rather than a testimony of belief. The author seeks to understand by the use of reason the meaning of human existence and the good which man can find in life."[1] And yet, somehow, the religious communities that have revered this book for millennia have found sustenance for their faith in it. Otherwise, it would never have been included in the Bible in the first place, and indeed it has played an important—even if not unproblematic—role in the religious reflection of the faithful throughout the centuries.

---

1. May and Metzger, *The Oxford Annotated Bible,* 805.

The hypothesis of the reading I wish to propose here is that Ecclesiastes is a very powerful, albeit somewhat indirect, testimony of faith. The philosophical reflections it offers, leading always inescapably to the conclusion that all is vanity, are meant to show not the futility of life itself but rather the inability of philosophy to understand it. They thereby point beyond philosophy to faith as necessary to any adequate understanding of the world and of human existence. The reader must therefore allow for a reversal of the book's overt assertions—a reversal that is realized by a subtle rhetorical strategy. The effectual meaning of the book is to be gathered not directly from what it affirms, namely, that "all is vanity," but rather from the manifest vanity of philosophical reasoning itself: such thinking cannot discover any lasting value in existence and therefore keeps coming back compulsively to the conclusion that all is vanity. It is the vanity of *philosophy*—and of everything as seen in the view of philosophy—that is played out and proved by the text's repeated, syllogistic assertions of "vanity." These assertions display *their own* vain absurdity. The text exhibits the fallacy of philosophy as a merely human endeavor to know all things in their true meaning and purport ("All things have I seen in the days of my vanity," 7:15) and consequently to be the master of one's own life. What presumably has always been felt, at least obscurely, by those who read the book through the lens of their religious faith, is that it is a *reductio ad absurdum* not of existence itself but of the type of egocentric philosophical ratiocination that sets itself up as the judge of life and its worth and then can find therein only vanity.

In this way, the book demonstrates the vanity not of life as God created it but of human reason in its presumption to know the meaning life and to understand the final end of things—which, so far as natural reason can see, can only be death. The Teacher's affirmations of vanity, for example, in 2:20–21 or 7:15, are subtly undercut by an irony that exposes these statements themselves—and the form of judgment they represent—as vain. We cannot but notice, for example, the self-enclosed, self-referential style of the Teacher's circuit of reasoning. He quotes himself in a self-satisfied tone, even in declaring his deep dissatisfaction: "I said to myself, 'I have acquired great wisdom, surpassing all who were over Jerusalem before me; and my mind has had great experience of wisdom and knowledge'" (1:16). That is certainly a dangerous affirmation to make about oneself. By whose standards does the speaker esteem himself so savant? He has evidently assumed his own standards and judgment as definitive and absolute. In the context of the whole Bible, which constantly inculcates reliance on God rather than on oneself, we cannot but sense the perhaps inadvertent irreverence and arrogance of this blind self-assurance.

What better illustration of how it is folly to be wise—as Alexander Pope was to write—than this sort of solipsistic dialogue of the self with itself. The circularity of this reasoning is made explicit at the linguistic surface by a rhetoric of talking to oneself: "I said to myself, 'Come now, I will make a test of pleasure; enjoy yourself.' But again, this also is vanity" (2:1). In this way, "Solomon" in his greatness, as described in chapter 2, comes across as afflicted by colossal conceit and self-absorption, and his pessimism can be seen to be a consequence not of the order of things in the universe but of his narrowly self-centered perception of it—as representative of human egocentricity in general.

The existential sickness unto death expressed in Ecclesiastes's philosophy of despair, then, is not shown to be the only—or even the natural or necessary—response to life as it is given in the human condition. It is the outcome rather of the Teacher's own all too typically human egocentrism and reliance on self rather than on God as the foundation for his judgment. The vainly egotistical logic of the Teacher's reasonings communicates to everything it touches a pessimistic spin. Thus the fact that, upon dying, we leave all that we have accumulated to someone else who did not labor for it provides one more reason for despondency in this characteristically self-involved utterance: "So I turned and gave my heart up to despair concerning all the toil of my labors under the sun, because sometimes one who has toiled with wisdom and knowledge and skill must leave all to be enjoyed by another who did not toil for it. This also is vanity and a great evil" (2:20–21). All this labor and toil of the ego is shown quite conclusively to be vanity. The speaker wants to possess the fruits of those labors himself rather than let them be inherited by someone else. More generally, he wants to be his own master and *raison d'être* rather than acknowledging that the purpose of his existence is determined by a radically other being, namely, God, who surpasses his understanding and who beholds the true meaning of things, even where the preacher himself can see no meaning at all.

The book opens with observation of the cycles of time from a detached point of view and advances the judgment that "all is vanity" and a striving after wind. But what really proves vain, by the showing of these circuitous verses, is the self-referential pattern of reasoning itself: futile is the endeavor to judge life by the standards of human reason rather than adapting and adjusting reason to life as it is given in the Creation. It is the philosopher's detached remoteness, pretending to survey all things and to sift their meaning, as if from the omniscient vantage point of God, which makes them appear vain to him. As actually lived, and thus as seen from within time and its involvements, things are not vain at all. When things are done in their own proper time, they are filled with poignancy and purpose. From this point of view, everything, whether happy or sad, is just as it should be:

> To everything there is a season,
>
> And a time to every purpose under the heaven:
>
> A time to be born, and a time to die;
>
> A time to plant, and a time to pluck up that which is planted;
>
> A time to kill, and a time to heal;
>
> A time to break down, and time to build up;
>
> A time to weep, and a time to laugh;
>
> A time to mourn, and a time to dance;
>
> A time to cast away stones, and a time to gather stones together;
>
> A time to embrace, and time to refrain from embracing;
>
> A time to get, and a time to lose;
>
> A time to keep, and a time to cast away;
>
> A time to rend, and a time to sew;
>
> A time to keep silence, and a time to speak;
>
> A time to love, and a time to hate;
>
> A time of war, and a time of peace. (3:1–8)

These verses express a spirit of acceptance of time and its cycles rather than of judgment and of what Nietzsche was later to call "revenge" against time and its "It was"—the ostensibly unchangeable fixity of the past (*The Gay Science,* Book IV, aphorism 341). They accept that man's consciousness is time-bound and that he must be guided by the times and seasons with their changes rather than endeavor to judge by any other standard of his own that presumes to transcend them. The temptation to do so is constant, yet the attempt is doomed to fail, for its time-boundedness marks the absolute difference between human and divine knowledge. As stated in verses following close upon those given above, "He"—that is, God—"has made everything suitable in his time; moreover he has put a sense of past and future into their minds, yet they cannot find out what God has done from the beginning to the end" (3:11). Human beings have "eternity" or "a sense of the past and the future" or "the world" (*ha-olam*) in their heart: they possess a faculty of reflection that enables them, in effect, to transcend the present and to synoptically overview the succession of times. Yet humans do not have the key to time's meaning, they cannot see beyond its furthest limits, so as to know the final purpose of things. They must accept time's terms, hence mortality. But once they do, they can indeed have much profit from life: "I know that there is nothing better for them than to be happy and enjoy themselves as long as they live" (3:12).

This optimistic morality, which is evidently in contradiction with the Teacher's pessimism, is explicitly articulated in clusters of verses and occasional passages that point up the limits of his rigorous philosophy of vanity. Life can be rapturously affirmed, even without reasons, by anyone who accepts to abide within its mortal limits: "In the day of prosperity be joyful, and in the day of adversity consider; God has made the one as well as the other, so that mortals may not find out anything that will come after them" (7:14). Only the last clause endeavors to snare what is a heartily positive, all-accepting outlook in the nets of nihilistic mistrust. An originally sanguine version could conceivably have been modified by an editorial intervention in order to jerk this verse back into line with the philosophy of pessimism expressed in the statement of vanity that frames the preacher's teaching as a whole. Originally the thought may have resembled that of another verse that stands as an unqualified affirmation of life without any reasons but rather simply as an immediate, indisputable perception: "Truly the light is sweet, and a pleasant thing it is for the eyes to behold the sun" (11:7). The following verse reads plausibly as a later addition in order to force this irrepressible effusion of cheerfulness back towards a formally negative conclusion: "But if a man live many years, and rejoice in them all; yet let him remember the days of darkness; for they shall be many. All that cometh is vanity" (11:8). Is there not something mechanical or perfunctory about this inevitable, obligatory melancholy?

The first thought—"Truly the light is sweet, and a pleasant thing it is for the eyes to behold the sun"—is pure joy, and it is simply given with no caveats. It is a joy not in anything produced by our own thought or possessed through our own labor. The Teacher, in typically human fashion, had attempted to construct his own happiness in life, and he found it a toilsome task and full of vexation. But this is because he tried to be the master of life and its joys and pains rather than accepting whatever comes as given from God, taking the good with the bad. What seems bad or unpleasant to us is evidently still good in the sight of God, which surpasses our own outlook. In fact, man's work on earth is not to be calculated and judged by us, but rather to be performed in a spirit of exhilaration in life and of open acceptance of its mystery. Then all is not vanity but is rather filled with significance that is perhaps sometimes terrible as well as delightful. But in any case, it is not experienced merely as vanity.

Chapter 11, on balance, suggests that one must live with confidence in life and its returns—"Cast thy bread upon the waters: for thou shalt find it after many days" (11:11)—and without worrying about or calculating the final outcome of it all, which, in any event, is unknowable to mortals. Too much worrying and reflection will rob one of vitality and, in effect, prevent one from living and producing:

> He that observeth the wind shall not sow;
> and he that regardeth the clouds shall not reap.
> As thou knowest not what is the way of the spirit,
> nor how the bones do grow in the womb
> of her that is with child:
> even so thou knowest not the works of God who maketh all.
> In the morning sow thy seed,
> and in the evening withhold not thine hand:
> for thou knowest not whether shall prosper,
> either this or that, or whether they both shall be alike good.
> (11:4–7)

Reason wants to see beyond time and keeps asking, what do you have in the end? To which the answer, of course, is nothing, nothing but death. Therefore, all is vanity. This is inevitably the answer for reason that reflects itself, by its powers of abstraction, out of the actual, living involvements of existence. And yet, life is full of immanent meaning for human beings involved in its manifold processes: "for everything there is a time . . ." In chapter 12, at the very climax of the book, even death—to take the most challenging theme of all to interpret in any perspective other than that of vanity—is viewed immanently as a process unfolding from within life. As such, far from reducing all to the one abstract significance of "vanity," death is full of untold, mysterious meaning as expressed by the many vital and vigorous suggestions of the poetry:

Remember now thy Creator in the days of thy youth, while the
evil days come not, nor the years draw nigh, when thou shalt say, I
have no pleasure in them; while the sun, or the light, or the moon,
or the stars, be not darkened, nor the clouds return after the rain:
In the day when the keepers of the house shall tremble, and the
strong men shall bow themselves, and the grinders cease because
they are few, and those that look out of the windows be darkened,
And the doors shall be shut in the streets, when the sound of the
grinding is low, and he shall rise up at the voice of the bird, and
all the daughters of musick shall be brought low; Also when they
shall be afraid of that which is high, and fears shall be in the way,
and the almond tree shall flourish, and the grasshopper shall be a
burden, and desire shall fail; because man goeth to his long home,
and the mourners go about the streets: Or ever the silver cord be
loosed, or the golden bowl be broken, or the pitcher be broken
at the fountain, or the wheel broken at the cistern. Then shall the
dust return to the earth as it was: and the spirit shall return unto
God who gave it. (12:1–7)

The "strong men" bowing down here represent the hunched–over
shoulders of old age; the few grinders ceasing to work, an advancing tooth-
lessness; the darkened windows, a loss of sight, and so on. For here we con-
template death not just as an absolute limit, but from within time. Hence
the piquant, humanly rich allegorical figure conveying an intimate sense of
the ailments of age, its dreary infirmities and ghastly disfigurements—yet
vividly pictured in their lively and stark significance and human drama.
The passage can inspire desire to live with redoubled intensity the limited
time that is given to mortals before the dimming and closing off of the
senses and slackening of the appetites (the loosening silver cord and the
broken golden bowl can be taken sexually, as Blake suggests in the "Motto"
to *The Book of Thel*), before the shakiness of the limbs of the elderly and the
lightness of their sleep broken at the sound of a bird. When death itself is
not simply reasoned about in the abstract as the final reduction to vanity,
but is viewed immanently and is lived through in the graphic unfolding of
its process of decline, it turns out to be very moving and expressive, full of
pathos and poetic meaning in every detail. It is not all pretty, but it is in any
case not just vanity.

Especially the poetry of chapters 3, 11, and 12, which are written
largely in verse form, expresses this alternative point of view. Such poetic
vision does not stand outside of life so as to judge it by rational, human
standards but is rather immersed within the stream of its continuing

process. Wisdom is conceived at the end of the book, in effect, as relational knowing: "Let us hear the conclusion of the whole matter: Fear God, and keep his commandments: for this is the whole duty of man" (12:13). Just as in Proverbs, "The fear of the Lord is the beginning of knowledge" (1:7). It is a right relationship with one's Maker, rather than howsoever ingenious insight acquired by one's own lights, that alone is apt to make a human being truly wise.

Although this "pious conclusion" has often been said to be tacked on in order to give an orthodox meaning to a rebellious book, it seems just as arguable that this conclusion somewhat more curtly and explicitly expresses what the book's poetry as a whole persuades us to believe. It may actually be certain pessimistic deductions and syllogisms that have been tacked on in search of "consistency" and due to fundamental lack of understanding of the book's poetic mode of argument and its deeply ironic rhetoric. Ultimately, this book means the opposite of what it repeatedly and programmatically says, for the philosophical statements discredit themselves: as the text performs them, they illustrate *their own* vanity. This performative reversal gives a measure of the freedom and flexibility that revelation takes on in the Writings. It suggests how the human voice can lend itself to becoming a vehicle of God's Word, in spite of and even *because of* its inability to directly state the truth of that Word. Precisely this inadequacy enables the truth about human limits to be revealed beyond what the words themselves can say.

Read in this way, this work is the converse of prophecy: it reveals by the unmistakable inadequacy and even irreverence of its human words rather than by the incontrovertible authority of direct divine speech. Human beings, except when inspired extraordinarily by God, do not see the world from a prophetic perspective—and knowing this is wisdom. As a profoundly ironic text turning on a rhetorically performed reversal, Ecclesiastes teaches us our human limits (together with God's infinite, incomprehensible superiority) and the necessity of acting on faith rather than just relying on our own reasoning. As such, and because it teaches this indirectly—not by means of pious statements but by their apparent opposite—Ecclesiastes has been wondrous in its workings and has been cherished by countless readers in all ages, perhaps especially by those struggling with doubt and yet arduously in search of faith.

III. The Song of the Senses

The Song of Songs has remained an enigma for scholarly efforts to define its original form and purpose. It is sometimes taken to be a dramatic poem, one which could be reconstructed by assigning groups of verses to a cast of characters including the Shulamite, King Solomon, and Choruses made up of the Brothers and Daughters of Jerusalem. Another hypothesis is that it is rather an anthology of love poems, all independent compositions.[2] In any case, the human voice breaks irrepressibly into a multiplicity of expressions in this work. The speakers in the Song are inherently multiple and differentiated, without any pre-established, unitary self-identity. The perennial question in interpretation of the Song of Songs is whether this multiplicity harmonizes into an ultimate unity that transcends its isolated ejaculations. If there is such a unity, furthermore, might it indicate a transcendent, divine love beyond all the merely sensual impulses that are so frankly expressed and made so palpably manifest? The context of the Song within the biblical canon has exerted constant pressure throughout the ages in precisely this direction of interpretation. Hence the persistent determination to read the Song as a dialogue between God and his people, or between Christ and the Church, the bridegroom and his bride, and therefore as a discourse revealing a love that is realized ultimately as a union of humanity with divinity. Such allegorical interpretation has kept the most celebrated exegetes—from Origen to Saint Bernard—busy for millennia producing massive volumes of commentary.[3]

I would like to be receptive to the intuitions on which this tradition of commentary is based and, at the same time, read the Song of Songs radically in its essence as poetry[4]—and therefore also as exceeding any particular confessional appropriation. Poetry in its intrinsic indeterminacy, given the characteristic polysemousness of metaphorical expression, signifies infinitely: taken to its limits, poetry opens itself to signifying the Infinite. It is, therefore, no accident that this love poetry has lent itself so well to being read as an allegory of divine, that is, of infinite Love. Perhaps all radically poetic language tends to speak of such Love. In an age in which

2. Robert, "Le genre littéraire du Cantique des Cantiques"; Falk, *Love Lyrics from the Bible*.

3. For contemporary transmissions and transformations of this tradition, see especially Jean-Louis Chrétien, *Symbolique du corps* and Anne–Marie Pelletier, *Lectures du Cantique des Cantiques*.

4. Cf. Hunt, *Poetry in the Song of Songs*.

poetic language is more often taken to be subversive of all unified order, it is important to recollect this potential of poetry for absolute meaning—or even perhaps for attaining an absolute beyond meaning, where sense turns into pure sensation. Poetry is this, too, especially when pursuing the Rimbaldian project announced in the famous "Lettres du voyant," according to which "The poet becomes a seer by a long, immense, and deliberate derangement *of all the senses*" ("Le poète se fait voyant par un long, immense et raisonné dérèglement de *tous les sens*").[5] But precisely its unruliness and spontaneity are laden with the suggestion that poetry's uncanny beauty and power devolve from a transcendent order which it expresses in a way that remains beyond rational calculation.

If the object of the Song of Songs is to express divine love exceeding human comprehension, it does so by representing an absolute degree of human or sensual love. One might speak here, with Luce Irrigaray, of a "sensible transcendental."[6] It is the limitlessness of the love in question precisely in its total sensual abandon, devoid of any specific doctrinal content, that makes it comparable to divine love. Love is absolute and its own authority in this universe. Love must be allowed absolute freedom to do its own pleasure, without being conditioned externally:

> I charge you, O ye daughters of Jerusalem,
> by the roes, and by the hinds of the field,
> that ye stir not up, nor awake my love, till he please. (3:5)

It is, furthermore, unabashedly sensual, sexual love that is being celebrated here. The allegorical veil of a highly figurative language, depicting, for example, the mound of Venus as a mountain of myrrh and frankincense, only makes more exquisite and provocative a dramatic and, above all, erotic climax such as the following:

> I sleep, but my heart waketh:
> it is the voice of my beloved that knocketh, saying,
> Open to me, my sister, my love, my dove, my undefiled:
> for my head is filled with dew,
> and my locks with the drops of the night.
> I have put off my coat; how shall I put it on?
> I have washed my feet; how shall I defile them?

5. Arthur Rimbaud, Letter to Paul Demeny, May 15, 1871. Such a conception of poetry is developed in theoretical terms by Julia Kristeva, *La révolution du langage poetique*.

6. See especially Irigaray's *Éthique de la différence sexuelle*.

My beloved put in his hand by the hole of the door,
and my bowels were moved for him.
I rose up to open to my beloved;
and my hands dropped with myrrh,
and my fingers with sweet smelling myrrh,
upon the handles of the lock. (5:2–5)

The unchecked exaltation of the senses, the uncircumscribed intensity of pure sensation, is the most appropriate human vehicle for expressing the unlimited intensity of divine love. Paradoxically, in this way the senses in their own purity and absoluteness can suggest what transcends sense-experience altogether. The experience of the senses is perhaps what comes closest in an analogical sense to the experience of God. The total exposure and vulnerability and the enrapturing ecstasy of sex have across untold ages and in numerous different art forms been seen as like the religious rapture of the direct experience of God. Bernini's sculpture, in the Cornaro chapel in Santa Maria della Vittoria in Rome, of Saint Teresa pierced by a glowing shaft and in an attitude often interpreted as expressing orgasm is emblematic of this surprising coincidence of spirituality with sensuality wrought to its uttermost.

If this unabashed sensuality is seen and admitted, the Song raises the question of the place of sensual love in the economy of redemption and salvation. The image of the love of the bridegroom for the bride and vice versa became, in fact, a canonical figure for divine love. It recurs in the penultimate chapter of the Book of Revelation, with "new Jerusalem, coming down from God out of heaven, prepared as a bride adorned for her husband" (21:2). Can precisely sensual attraction and erotic exultation become something holy? Without any special qualifications? Sensual love per se is life and energy, innocent of good and evil, and as such it is wholly "good" like Creation before the Fall. Sensation is per se infinite, in the sense that it is without conceptual definition and contour. It is precisely the unqualified, unlimited nature of this love as pure sensation that suggests and signifies divinity, the Infinite. And this significance of sensation is expressed best in poetry because of the latter's relative indeterminacy, its intentionality reaching beyond all that its words concretely and pragmatically designate.

The innocence presupposed by the unchecked, unselfconscious abandon to sensual excitement expresses itself further in a certain flouting of boundaries that normally demarcate legitimate from forbidden love. By virtue of poetic license, a certain ambiguously incestuous urge can be freely and innocently avowed:

> O that thou wert as my brother,
> That sucked the breasts of my mother!
> When I should find thee without, I would kiss thee;
> Yea, I should not be despised.
> I would lead thee, and bring thee into my mother's house,
> who would instruct me; I would cause thee to drink
> of spiced wine of the juice of my pomegranate. (8:1–2)

The same incestuous suggestion surfaces in the epithet "my sister, my bride," which occurs in 5:1 and 4:9—"You have ravished my heart, my sister, my bride, you have ravished my heart with a glance of your eyes . . . ." Such employment of "brother" and "sister" is perhaps just formulaic and customary, a literary convention for signifying closeness or affinity. Nevertheless, the straightforward literal sense also is released to work poetically on the imagination. The effect is to suggest that nothing is impure in this ideal garden of love and poetry. The universal desire moving towards unity, ultimately of all in one, knows no boundaries. Love, as return to origin—which is paradigmatically the case with love for God as the transcending of all separateness through the *unio mystica*—is inherently a sort of metaphysical incest. It is fulfilled here in the ultimate realization of an absolute poetry, where everything is totally open to everything else: indeed all things are ambiguously identified with one another. This becomes explicit and programmatic in Symbolist poetics, with Baudelaire and Mallarmé,[7] but it may be at work at some level in poetry generally and not least here in the poetry of the Song of Songs.

The elusiveness of this poem as a drama—the difficulty of pinning down the exact scenario and the *dramatis personae*—frees it from social and moral categories. It is the innocence of sensual love, pure sensation without reflection, as in the Garden of Eden, that makes it redolent of holiness. The indeterminacy of poetic language creates the possibility of undoing all constraints of law and social mores. Therefore language is completely freed and takes on a life of its own in this poem that upstages any field of reference to extra-linguistic realities. This is typical of poetic language, particularly at

---

7. I develop this idea in "The Linguistic Turning of the Symbol: Baudelaire and his French Symbolist Heirs," in *Baudelaire and the Poetics of Modernity;* now chapter 6 in *Secular Scriptures.*

its most flamboyant or baroque. The similes, being elaborate and somewhat far-fetched, tend to overpower what they stand for and so to catapult us into a realm of pure metaphor.

> Thy hair is a flock of goats,
> That lie along the side of Gilead.
> Thy teeth are like a flock of ewes,
> Which are come up from the washing;
> Whereof every one hath twins,
> And none is bereaved among them.
> Thy temples are a piece of pomegranate
> Behind thy veil. (6:5–7)

Many conceits, like the comparison of the neck to "the tower of David builded for an armoury, whereon there hang a thousand bucklers, all shields of mighty men" (4:4), by a certain ostentation and sometimes even preposterousness, highlight language itself as the main theme. Descriptions like "thy nose is as the tower of Lebanon / Which looketh toward Damascus" (7:4) no longer help us to visualize the referential object more exactly but rather substitute a new register of meaning for what is literally envisaged. The thematic object becomes a pretext for the image rather than the image being a means of representing its object.[8]

A taste for extravagance and luxurious stylization may be thought to belong in the first place simply to a certain oriental aesthetic that characterizes the poem. But the often somewhat shockingly non-naturalistic imagery makes sense also, if not in terms of the object, then at least in terms of emotions projected onto it. This holds, for example, in the description of the beloved woman as "terrible as an army with banners" (6:4, 10). Though the beloved is elsewhere described as in every way superlatively attractive and inviting, certainly there is something fearful in the experience of love and its overpowering passions that rob one of one's sovereignty and self-control and make one vulnerable.

In descriptions wrought to the breaking point, the poetic medium of the Song declares, finally, the ineffability of its subject.[9] The obvious stretch-

8. Robert Alter suggests that in the comparisons in which this desire is expressed, the second term of the comparison flaunts metaphor "by pushing its frame of reference into the foreground" (*Art of Biblical Poetry,* 197) rather than using metaphor to point to and sharpen its referent. This analysis follows I. A. Richards' theory of metaphorical language in *The Philosophy of Rhetoric.*

9. Frisch, "Song of Solomon: The Allegorical Imperative" similarly draws an inference

ing of the imagery to an extreme hints at the poet's impotence to adequately express the theme. This could hardly help but be the case where this theme is divine love. The absolute experience of love, represented by pure sensuality, fosters an absolute experience of language, which in its purity is silence, the silence of pure sensation. And that is sacred.

IV. The Psalms as Israel's Hymnal

Perhaps the most intimately human language addressed to God in the Bible is found in the Psalms.[10] "Psalm" means "song of praise," from the Hebrew *Tehillim*, "Praises." The praise motif can occur in conjunction with many different themes. Psalm 18, for example, gathers images of both the Creator God of Genesis and the Redeemer God of Exodus into its motives for praise and blessing of the Almighty. God lays the foundation of the earth (18:15) and saves his people (18:43), and for this he is extolled (18:44). This type of rehearsal of the Creation story and the Exodus history—the founding narratives of the Hebrew faith—reflects a pragmatic communicative situation (*Sitz-im-Leben*), namely, liturgical recitation.[11]

The Psalms very often manifest liturgical designs, and this is the most important key to understanding them in terms of their genre.[12] The liturgical context sometimes even shows through the text, for example, in Psalm 24:

> Lift up thy heads, O ye gates;
> and be ye lift up, ye everlasting doors;
> and the King of glory shall come in.

These lines, repeated verbatim as a kind of refrain, belong verisimilarly to a religious procession, presumably one bearing the Ark of the Covenant through the gates of the temple precinct. Similar explicit references to the place of worship are found in Psalm 122, for example, which bears traces of a pilgrimage:

---

from the poem's "riot of images" to the unspeakability of "God himself, whom all metaphors merely conceal" (103). Frisch also stresses the irrepressibility of the allegorical drive.

10. Among contemporary readings, I find this emphasis in Sarna, *On the Book of Psalms: Exploring the Prayers of Ancient Israel* and *Songs of the Heart: An Introduction to the Book of Psalms*; and in Anderson, *Out of the Depths: The Psalms Speak for us Today*.

11. See Mowinckel, *The Psalms in Israel's Worship*.

12. Gunkel, *Einleitung in die Psalmen*.

I was glad when they said unto me,
Let us go into the house of the Lord;
Our feet shall stand within thy gates, O Jerusalem,

and in Psalm 84:

How amiable are thy tabernacles, O Lord of hosts!

Frequently such liturgical functions can be descried thinly veiled beneath the verses. The genre of the psalm as such may even be considered as fundamentally liturgical and cultic in nature. Of course, the prayer of the soul to God in the Psalms can sometimes be very personal and private, but more typically it is rather choral and communal. The liturgical purpose of the Psalms determines, accordingly, their generally somewhat conventional style. Audacities of an original and personal style are not well suited to collective worship and are better adapted to the uncanny, idiosyncratic voice of one of the prophets. We must imagine that most of the psalms were sung and prayed in community and were transmitted orally long before they were ever written down.[13]

The Psalms have been read in Christian churches since antiquity as all about Christ, the Savior, the Son of God. They have been the most intensely prayed of books in the daily divine office of monasteries for two millennia. Christological readings powerfully illustrate how interpretation centers and focuses—and can give new meaning to—antecedent traditions. Psalms 2 and 110 are among the psalms that lend themselves best to this sort of re-reading. When the psalmist, traditionally identified as King David, sings, "The Lord said unto my lord, / 'Sit at my right hand / until I make thine enemies thy footstool,'" the second lord mentioned here as the speaker's Lord (the speaker being identified traditionally with King David) is taken by Christian exegetes to be the second person of the Trinity, and the victories alluded to are interpreted as the spiritual triumph of Christ.

Since Jesus himself prayed the Psalms, in some instances these reframings of sense have a Scriptural warrant. The incipit of Psalm 22, "My God, my God, why hast thou forsaken me?" is well known as containing words spoken by Christ on the Cross. Hence the transfer to the Gospel narrative relating Christ's Crucifixion of details such as the following:

. . . the assembly of the wicked have enclosed me:
they pierced my hands and my feet.

13. Westermann, *Ausgewählte Psalmen*, 13.

I may tell all my bones:
they look and stare upon me.
They part my garments among them,
and cast lots upon my vesture. (Ps 22:16–18)

These pitiful laments express the utter despair of abandon that Christ had to undergo in order to gather the whole of human suffering, experienced all the way down to its lowest depths, into his redemptive act. What is not always realized is that recitation of the opening verse—the *incipit*—of a psalm was a Hebrew practice for invoking the psalm in its entirety. Since this psalm goes on to sing praises to God for his saving actions, the cry of despair is already intrinsically linked with a celebration of God's glory and ultimate triumph.

Certain of the Psalms have a life not only in liturgy but also in later literature. For example, Psalm 23, "The Lord is my shepherd, I shall not want," is a founding text of the tradition of pastoral poetry, notably in England. This tradition is taken up memorably by Blake's verses:

And did those feet in ancient time
Walk upon England's mountains green:
And was the holy Lamb of God
On England's pleasant pastures seen! (Preface to *Milton*)

If in the Psalms the human soul or the people are speaking and addressing God, this is a dialogue that goes on everywhere in all ages. The Psalms carry the inspiration of the Bible forward lyrically into the life of all people who become its heirs.

Literary artifice marries the psalms in all times with the theme of the Word. Particularly the divine Word of Creation is celebrated in Psalm 19. It envisions the heavens as "declaring the glory of God" and listens to their language resounding throughout the earth. But then in verse 7, without transition, the object celebrated metamorphoses from the word to the law: "The law of the Lord is perfect, converting the soul." Psalm 119 goes further in this praise and displays passionate love for the Law, which is felt not as an imposition but as a gift enabling Israel to live in intimate fellowship with God: "O how I love thy law!" (119:97). This psalm is intricately structured as an alphabetical acrostic. Each of its twenty-two stanzas consists in eight lines all beginning with the same letter of the alphabet. Moreover, each successive stanza of the poem rehearses a series of eight different names for the law—"ordinances," "statutes," "precepts," "judgments," "commandments," "decrees," also "word" and "promise"—one in each verse. Each name bears a different nuance, and all contribute to a great symphonic celebration of the Law: it is as precious as the gift of life itself, for in it the Lord gives himself to his people.

Psalms is the most fundamental and most frequented book of the Bible as it has been used in worship and prayer in religious communities throughout the ages. Psalms more than all other books has functioned literally as the Word of God engraved upon the hearts of millions who have consecrated their lives to the unceasing praise of divinity. The poetic nature of the Psalms suits them for this role as the daily bread of the faithful. Especially their poetry renders the divine Word unforgettable, inspiring, and up-building, and thereby makes the Psalms a staple of spiritual nourishment for the soul.

V. Job and Poetry

The drift of the Book of Job is to suggest that in the writing of the Bible, just as in the act of Creation by the divine Word, there is something which humans cannot comprehend. For all the co-inherence of human and divine agency in revelation, there is in divinity necessarily an excess to all that can be humanly grasped and transmitted. It is symbolized by the violence that the text embodies and expresses, especially in the turbulent Whirlwind out of which the divine Voice speaks, as well as in the daunting figures of the Leviathan, the crocodile, and the hippopotamus, representing unmasterable natural forces. The answer to the questions raised by Job is given only in poetry as a vision of the sublime nature and awesomeness of the creation, not in any precepts or principles that human reason can grasp. In Robert Alter's words, "creation can perhaps be sensed but not encompassed by the mind."[14] Rather than receiving an answer to the questions he poses, Job is brought face to face with his limits and, consequently, with the presumptuousness of the questions he asks. This is the sense in which, at the end, he "sees" (42:4). He sees that creation and its governing principle are beyond the measure of his understanding.

The poetry of Job aspires to open up allusively, beyond human ken, the infinite perspective of God, who as Creator saw all that he had made and saw that it was good. To man's rationalistic, egocentric view, this is not evident. On the contrary, often all appears to be vanity, as to the Teacher in

14. Alter, *Art of Biblical Poetry*, 110.

Ecclesiastes. Just as in that book, here also poetry is deployed in an attempt to transcend the ordinary limits of human vision and perception. This attempt aspires by human means—marshalling all the resources that literary talent and technique can command—to approach the prophetic perspective from which God speaks.

The poetry of chapters 38–41, in which the Voice speaks out of the Whirlwind, compared with the rest of the book, are of an originality in conception and expression such as to justify the claim of God to absolute authority over the Creation. There is a certain violence in Creation as an act of dividing: some sort of tearing apart is the condition of existence of everything, including man, who is torn from his mother's womb at birth. The divinely prophetic and oracular poetry of Job embodies this principle, revealing the incomprehensible goodness of the Creation, showing forth the majesty and authority of the universal order that exceeds all human moral categories. Above and beyond any reasoned judgment hovers the experience of awe in contact with the divine, to which the text witnesses by virtue of its incomparable poetry. A concrete symbol of this rears up in the Leviathan, who is in every way beyond man's control, as is stressed in the rhetorical question: "Can you draw out Leviathan with a fish-hook?" This majestic monster is "king over all the sons of pride."

Job is widely recognized as a surpassingly sublime poetic masterpiece that warrants being pondered at length in all its exquisite details. A microscopic analysis of its literary mechanisms and rhetorical techniques is being pursued today most comprehensively and innovatively by C. L. Seow. Seow demonstrates anatomically exactly how Job has been able to attain the rank universally accorded it thanks to to the synergism of the work's poetry and its theological insights: "The book of Job is, thus, an exquisite work of literary art, indeed, the very best in the Bible. It is also a remarkably rich theological work."[15] Seow analyzes in exhaustive detail the poetic effects of the language. My discussion, in contrast, will have to settle for these summary indications of how Job contributes to understanding the poetic nature of religious revelation that is being explored here through reading the Bible as a humanities text. A preeminent place in such a reading must be accorded finally to the Gospel—as we will see in the next and last chapter.

15. Seow, *Job 1–21*, 87.

VI. Theoretical–Theological Conclusion

These are but summary indications of how the Writings contribute to an understanding of the poetic nature of religious revelation as it has been developed here through reading some books from the biblical Writings as humanities texts. Such a reading has been proposed not against the claim of these writings to be divine revelation but rather as a way of suggesting what this might mean in human and in literary terms. Such a reading is "theological," not in a dogmatic sense but, instead, in its astonishing discovery of *theos* as inhering in *logos*. A certain sense of divinity can be found reflected already simply in the language that humans use to express the deepest roots of their existence and consciousness. A transcendent reality or sphere of experience has been discovered particularly in the unfathomable opening of meaning in poetry to a dimension of indeterminacy. Theology is then proposed as a discourse that interprets this dimension imaginatively through exploring the existential experience vis-à-vis an unutterable ground or groundlessness—in any articulable terms—of our being and of all that is.

Kindred reflections along the lines of a literary theology contemplating and speculating on certain inherently theological latencies of language have been proposed notably by Paul Ricoeur in his reading of selected texts from the Bible in *Thinking Biblically*. Ricoeur similarly emphasizes "those quite striking features of indetermination," which give poetic language a sort of transcendence of all pragmatic contexts of communication. With reference specifically to the Song of Songs, he writes of "the tendency of the whole metaphorical interplay unfolded by the poem to free itself from its proper referential, that is, sexual, function."[16] This enables him to valorize the ancient and medieval allegorical interpretations of the poem (which are typically dismissed in modern historical-critical interpretation) as nevertheless pertinent reinvestments of the semantic potential of the poem and its metaphors in other, later historical and interpretive contexts.

Ricoeur refers to an "enclave of innocence" in the Song of Songs in which erotic love can connect itself with the "theologically approved" innocence of Genesis 2 and specifically with man's jubilation over woman whom God has made from him and then given to him to be his companion (2:23). This intertextual linking of Song of Songs with the story of the Creation of

16. Ricoeur and Lacoque, *Thinking Biblically*, 268.

woman suggests "the theological character of these two texts where God is not named or referred to."[17]

Thus Ricoeur, too, proposes a "theological" reading that conjugates ancient allegorical tradition with modern "naturalistic" readings of the book as simply an erotic dramatic poem. Its theological import is found within the poem's own autonomous and secular meaning as literature, but this meaning cannot be narrowly identified with any literal sense fixed by the supposedly original intention of the author(s) as it might be reconstructed by historical-critical methods. Instead, the poetry opens up a space of indetermination, which is the space that theology can interpret most intriguingly—with its self-subverting reference to an infinite God who remains always indeterminable in human language and consciousness. This "space" could also be conceived of as a "moment" that calls to be interpreted theologically, a moment of unlimited openness in the realization of the meaning of the text that allows it to be informed by relation to God, to the Infinite—or, equivalently, by infinite relations.

Ricoeur finds in the Song of Songs "a reconciliation between the sexual and the sacred" (298) and therefore also between the secular and the theological. He also concurs with the general approach being advocated in these pages in finding, beyond literary form, something that literature cannot convey except by canceling itself out and gesturing toward what is beyond logos: "reread in light of Genesis, the Song of Songs becomes a religious text insofar as we can hear in it the word of a silent, unnamed God, who is not discerned owing to the force of attestation of a love caught up in itself."[18] *Theos* is thus revealed as *logos* but also as always finally beyond *logos*: the mystery of the Father remains intact even in the revelation of the Word in the Son. This has been the "spirit" of the Hebrew Scriptures all along in their forcing the word to its limits and opening it to its own unfathomable beyond. This Spirit will be revealed in its full purport as divine Person in the word of the Gospel.

17. Ibid., 299.
18. Ibid., 298.

CHAPTER 6

The Gospel Truth: Personal Knowing and Miracle

I. An Uncanny Literary Genre

AT FIRST GLANCE, THE Gospel would seem to be a kind of biography, the life-story of Jesus of Nazareth. Moreover, to the extent that it purports to be a true story about events among a certain people in a particular historical time and place, it might also be assimilated superficially to history. In fact, much research into the Gospels has traditionally taken the form of the search for "the historical Jesus."[1] But these resemblances to other genres are deceptive, for the Gospel is in crucial respects *sui generis*. Gospel, considered as a literary genre, is not to be confounded with history or biography. Its purpose is not to recount the facts of Jesus's life per se, but to show what he meant for his disciples. Specifically, it shows how he revealed God to them in himself and thereby became their Savior. The Gospel witnesses to the power of Jesus to transform human lives and give them a new meaning. Gospel means literally "good news" (from Old English *god,* "good," and *spel*, "message" or "story"—like *Spiel* in German, used also in English: "a long spiel"). Indeed, it is good news that is meant to change people's lives:

---

1. Schweitzer, *The Quest for the Historical Jesus*. Contemporary continuations of this quest include John Dominic Crossan, *The Historical Jesus: The Life of a Mediterranean Jewish Peasant* and John P. Meier, *Jesus: A Marginal Jew. Rethinking the Historical Jesus*. David Friedrich Strauss's landmark *Das Leben Jesu* (1846) inaugurated the modern critical approach to such studies.

it proclaims a message of salvation rather than simply telling a story or a history for its own sake.

If the Gospels presented only the objective facts of Jesus's historical existence, they would not be able to say what is most important about him, for that is revealed only by his significance in the lives of the people whom he meets and who believe in him. It is his life-transforming power for the individuals who were changed by their belief in him that is supremely important, indeed miraculous. His followers were given new hope and were empowered to love in previously unattainable ways, ways for which they could not possibly have accounted otherwise. A purely factual account of Jesus's life—one hundred percent certain and demonstrated—would never be able to witness to the experience of this sort of power. A history could, at most, tell us about a man, whereas those who believed in Jesus personally perceived and experienced God. The idea that Jesus was a divine being, the Son of God—how could that ever be an observable fact and be recorded as such? How can such a conviction even be meaningful, except within the context of a personal relationship? If you look, you see a man. And if you insist on looking for objective, empirical proof of his being something else, you will never know what Jesus meant to those who knew him and followed him and loved him and believed in him and found in him their salvation.

To appreciate the Gospels accurately, even just as literature, we need to read them not as transparent to the historical Jesus but as testimonies of faith.[2] This makes it to a large degree futile to inquire: Did it really happen that way? What is being recorded fundamentally is how Jesus was *experienced*. To understand the Gospels as gospel—as the unique literary form and genre of religious testimony that they are—we need to ask instead: What meaning does that which is recounted have for those who experienced and perhaps *still* experience it? This is the meaning that can be interpreted and re-experienced as true in the present by readers in all ages, hence also by us still today. The Gospel is based on witness to purportedly historical happenings, yet it is fully unveiled never as naked history but rather always only for those who have made the commitment and decision of faith. Indeed, if humanities texts generally give us history and tradition always mediated by present reality and beliefs, this is acutely true in the case of the Gospels. For intrinsic to the Gospels as a genre is a further purpose beyond simply recording something that happened in the past: they

2. This is emphasized provocatively by the approach of Bultmann, *Theology of the New Testament*.

deliver their testimony in order that the reader or hearer of the word of the Gospel might believe in turn and be saved (John 20:31). Their message is directed towards an actualization of God's saving grace through Jesus in the lives of hearers and readers *now*, in the present tense of the Gospel as it is proclaimed, even if it is only being read in private to oneself.

If the Gospel is also in some sense a history, it is best understood as a *prophetic* type of history. For what is at stake is a living of history in the present and in light of a divine revelation of its meaning. Such revelation takes up a point of view outside the sequence of past events, one not attainable from within the series. The Gospels are indeed prophetic in the way that the whole Bible is prophetic, namely, in the sense that by recounting history they reveal something beyond history, what in a certain traditional language of faith can be called eternity. This is something which cannot be grasped as an objective fact in the order of the past or the future: it can only be lived and fathomed in the infinite freedom and openness of the present. As such, it is not fully formed and determinate but is rather in the process of determining all facts in their deepest significances. History in this way opens to "eternity." But this eternal dimension of significance to human life cannot be experienced as anything positively given. It is projective rather than positive, and it claims the whole individual in the intimate sphere of personal experience and decision. The "revelation of Jesus Christ" cannot be approached without such directly personal engagement.

To this extent, it is clear that the Gospel concerns what we have called personal knowing.[3] It is fundamentally not about facts but about their significance. It aims at opening up personal lives to possibilities beyond their parameters as ordinarily delineated and perceived. The knowledge of Jesus, in particular of Jesus as God, is inseparable from what people experience *about themselves* in relation to him. This experience occurs in the present and as decisive for the whole of their lives projected into the future without limit—and, in this sense, for all eternity.

To appreciate the different sorts of personal significance that can be conveyed by the Gospel as a genre, it is important to distinguish a variety of sub-genres operating within it. Examples of these sub-genres include the miracle story, the controversy (debates of Jesus against the scribes and Pharisees, for instance), and the parable.

---

3. An illuminating discussion of some of the wider epistemological ramifications of such knowing is Polanyi, *Personal Knowledge: Towards a Post-Critical Philosophy*.

A parable is a comparison developed in story form, usually to induce the auditor to make a judgment on himself—or herself.[4] The parable told by the prophet Nathan to David in 2 Samuel 12 illustrates this well. It is told as a means of stirring up David's conscience against himself for having had Uriah the Hittite placed in the front lines of battle to be killed, so that he, David, might possess Uriah's wife, Bathsheba. Nathan recounts that a rich man, in order to dress a meal for a wayfarer, instead of using his own livestock took from a poor man his ewe lamb, his one and only, which he carried in his bosom. When David's indignation is kindled, provoking him to cry out angrily for the offender's death, Nathan concludes dramatically: "Thou art the man!"

This example vividly illustrates how the effectual meaning of a parable arises out of and speaks into the specific situation of its hearers. These situations actually change in the course of transmission of the Gospels. Especially the conclusions or lessons drawn from parables tend to shift from being about the Kingdom of God—when Jesus tells them to the crowds—to being about Jesus himself when they are told by the Gospel writers. In the light of Easter, their sense is transformed from being theological to being Christological. They may even become ecclesiological in the light of Pentecost, when the Holy Spirit is bestowed from heaven in order to constitute the Church on earth (Acts 2:1–41). In such repurposing, for example, the marriage-feast parable addressed to the Pharisees in Matthew 22:1–14 is taken by Luke 14:15–24 as addressed to Christians. Whereas for Jesus the good news was the advent of the Kingdom of God, for the writers of "the Gospel of Jesus Christ" (Mark 1:1), Jesus himself becomes the good news. He is himself the central event of the new world that he announces, which may not be how he originally intended it. And it is an even further extrapolation to understand the wedding banquet to be the Church, which did not yet exist at the time of Jesus's original telling of the parable.

In their quest for the historical Jesus, scholars seek to reconstruct Jesus's preaching and ministry as it took place around AD 30. However, this is only one of several types of study of the Gospels, each endeavoring to gain access to a different level of their meaning and significance for subsequent generations. Another type of study focuses on the stage immediately after Jesus's ministry—on the oral elaboration of the Jesus tradition, from

4. Hence the "performative" aspect of biblical parables that is analyzed in sophisticated theoretical terms by J. Hillis Miller, "Parable and Performative in the Gospels and in Modern Literature." Miller also relates biblical parables to parables in secular literature by the likes Kafka and Kleist.

about AD 30 to 50. This material is studied particularly by the discipline of *Form Criticism*, which undertakes to reconstruct the *kerygma*, the essential proclamation of the Christian message of salvation. Form Criticism also endeavors to individuate and study the liturgy and catechisms of the earliest churches as transmitted in oral forms before being deposited in the documents of the New Testament and apocrypha.[5]

After this period, the first written traditions would have begun to take shape, and attempts to isolate them constitute another discipline known as *Source Criticism*. This discipline offers, for example, the hypothesis of a Q document (from German *Quelle*—source) comprising the sayings of Jesus common to Matthew and Luke but not found in Mark. Such a text seems to have been available to Matthew and Luke, since they repeat large sections of Jesus's teaching, agreeing with each other almost verbatim, although also with certain characteristic inflections of their own. Then sometime after AD 70 the written Gospels began to appear, and it is the business of *Redaction Criticism* to establish the derivations and lines of transmission of the manuscripts. Thus, in summary, "higher criticism" of the Bible breaks down into the following basic types of study correlated with successive phases in the formation of Gospel tradition:

			Manuscript
Jesus's Life	Oral Traditions	Written Traditions	Transmission
_____ 30	_____ 50	_____ 70	_____ AD
Historical Research	Form Criticism	Source Criticism	Redaction Criticism

This diachronic break-down traverses and stratifies the multiplicity of perspectives built into the four-fold canonical narration of the Gospel events and discourses.

---

5. A landmark work in this field is Martin Dibelius, *Die Formgeschichte des Evangeliums*.

II. Multifaceted Narration and Nuance
in the Experience of Truth

Using these sorts of criticism as tools, we can pay attention to how each of the Gospel writers writes about Jesus, and we can discover the significance that the traditions conveying Jesus's words and deeds had for the communities to which they belonged. For all the Gospel writers, that significance was that he was divine, and thus a miracle. Their lives were changed by him: they experienced redemption and salvation. But it is also possible to finely distinguish between the various writers and their very distinct experiences of Jesus, reflecting their different communities and cultural backgrounds, as well as their different theological agendas.

The Gospel according to Matthew is characterized, in the first place, by its conspicuous Jewishness. It was evidently written by and for Christians converted from Judaism. This appears from the outset in its special emphasis on genealogy and on Jesus's Davidic ancestry. Whereas Mark declares Jesus in his opening sentence to be the "son of God," Matthew opens by identifying Jesus as "the Messiah, the son of David." The first two chapters of Matthew, moreover, establish the pattern of reading every detail of Jesus's life as a fulfillment of Old Testament prophecy. This can be verified for events of the Gospel from the virgin birth of the Messiah—understood as having been foretold by Isaiah (7:14)—to his coming out of Bethlehem, as predicted by Micah (5:2), to the going down to Egypt, which Matthew links to a verse of Hosea: "Out of Egypt I have called my son" (1:11). Similarly, the slaughter of the innocents is read by Matthew (2:18) in correspondence with the weeping and lamentation in Ramah of Rachel for her children, spoken of by Jeremiah (31:15).

This pattern continues throughout the Gospel according to Matthew, with its repeated references the Jewish Scriptures, most often to Isaiah and the psalms. Such references, used as proof texts, are much more insistent in Matthew's version of the Gospel. The procedure becomes fully explicit when, for example, Matthew adds to an account of Jesus's miraculous healings: "This was to fulfill what had been spoken through the prophet Isaiah, 'He took our infirmities and bore our diseases'" (8:17). The same appeal to fulfillment of Isaiah's prophecies is made with reference to the chosen servant of the Lord and the oracle "I will put my Spirit upon him" in 12:17 (see, further, 4:14–16; 12:17–21; 13:35; 21:4–5; 27:9–10). Other clear indications of intimate involvement in Jewish affairs and their rival communities are the mission to Israel (10:6, 23), the story of the Canaanite woman (15:21–28), and the bitterness against the scribes and Pharisees (23:1–36; 12:1–14, etc.). At Jesus's Roman trial, Matthew adds the dream of Pilate's wife, thus deepening the guilt of the Jews as contravening a supernatural sign.

Sharply polemical against the unconverted Jewry of his day, Matthew's message is that Jesus is the fulfillment of the Law and the Prophets represented symbolically by Moses and Elijah, with whom Jesus appears transfigured on Mount Tabor. His face shines like the sun (17:2), just as did Moses's when he came down from Mount Sinai, bearing the tablets of the Law (Exod 34:29–35). This hints that Jesus recapitulates in his own life the history of the Israelites coming up out of Egypt and wandering forty years in the desert. His forty days fasting in the wilderness, where he is tempted by the devil (chapter 4), are immediately followed by the proclamation in the Sermon on the Mount, starting from chapter 5, of what in effect is a new covenant with God that fulfills the covenant made with Moses on Mount Sinai. In showing that the revelation of God is now fully vested in Jesus, Matthew nevertheless always carefully articulates the emergence of the new faith from the matrices of Judaism.

The Gospel according to Matthew is also distinguished as characteristically Jewish by the weight it gives to Jesus's teachings. His quintessentially rabbinical activity accords priority to the word, just as in the priestly story of the Creation in Genesis. More about Jesus's teaching is learned from Matthew than from any other Gospel writer. The teachings are concentrated into five great discourses (echoing the five-fold division of the books of Moses in the Pentateuch) that define the basic structure of this Gospel: the Sermon on the Mount in chapters 5–7; the commissioning of the disciples sent upon missions in chapter 10; seven parables of the kingdom of heaven in chapter 13; the rule of life for a community of disciples in chapter 18:1–20; and the apocalyptic discourse in chapters 24–25. The alternation of such discursive passages with narrative sequences is repeated throughout this Gospel as a whole. This divides the Gospel according to Matthew roughly into words and deeds: Jesus's preaching is followed by his enactment of the Kingdom of God (again paralleling the Creation paradigm: "And God said . . . and it was so").

The greatest of these discourses is the Sermon on the Mount, in which Jesus takes up and fulfills the teaching of the Law delivered by Moses from Mount Sinai. It begins with the beatitudes, which define a new kind of existence still immersed in the suffering of the world and yet placed also in relation to God and therefore "blessed." The beatitudes condense the core meaning and message of the Gospel and present it as an intensification and interiorization—but not an abrogation—of the Jewish Law and Scriptures. This is stated explicitly in the ensuing antitheses of chapter 5, beginning: "Think not that I am come to destroy the law or the prophets; I have come not to destroy but to fulfill" (5: 17).

A related distinguishing characteristic of Matthew among the Gospels is that the role of the Church is particularly pronounced. As the so-called "ecclesiological Gospel," Matthew bears the communitarian stamp of its Jewish origins. Its religion is conceived as the religion of a people. The fundamental experience of the Messiah occurs particularly in community worship. Indeed, Matthew's Jesus all along is—far more than just the man Jesus peregrinating around Palestine—the Risen Lord celebrated in the liturgy. All these distinctive traits, and the biases they embody, come out by comparison of the accounts of given incidents and exchanges with the other synoptic writers, each marked by its own specific theology and cultural background.

Whereas Mark leads us to discover first the man Jesus of Nazareth, Matthew presents the glorified Lord right from the prostrations of the Magi in adoration before the infant Jesus ("they knelt down and paid him homage," 2:11). The same gesture is repeated in closing this Gospel of the risen Christ with the disciples' prostration before the resurrected Jesus on the mountain in Galilee (28:17). Matthew's Jesus, moreover, is hieratic and solemn. He has a plethora of titles such as "King of Israel," "Governor," "Son of David," "King of the Jews," "Son of Abraham," and even his name "Jesus" is explained as meaning "God saves" (1:21) At his Jewish trial, Jesus foretells his coming in glory as the Son of Man. Jesus presents himself, moreover, explicitly as the beloved Son of his Father (11:27) and is repeatedly recognized as such by his disciples (14: 33; 16: 16), whereas in Mark the disciples never seem able to grasp his messianic identity.

Matthew eliminates the emotion and ignorance attributed to Jesus by Mark. Jesus's impotence as a prophet without honor in his own country ("he could there do no mighty work") according to Mark 6:5 is attenuated by Matthew to the acknowledgment: "And he did not many mighty works there because of their unbelief" (13:58). Matthew consistently accentuates Jesus's power. Matthew's Passion narrative (chapters 26–27) begins with Jesus's foretelling of his Crucifixion. From this point forward, Jesus is in control of the unfolding drama. He interprets the woman's pouring of costly ointment on his head in a house in Bethany as an anointing for his burial (26:6–12). In this, he resembles a priest celebrating the sacrifice of the Mass. The last supper is framed by Jesus's announcement of Judas's betrayal and of Peter's denial of him. He is conscious of himself as fulfilling the Scripture (26:31). The agony in the garden of Gethsemane shows Jesus's human side and vulnerability, though he is still master of the situation, un-like his sleep-prone disciples, to whom he is able to announce, just before the event, that his betrayer is at hand (26:45–46). Even when he is arrested, Jesus has the power to summon twelve legions of angels, but he declines to use it (26:53) and rather practices the non-resistance that he has preached.

Matthew also streamlines the miracle stories, eliminating much re-alistic detail and presenting the disciples as much more like Christians of his own time, so as to suggest how Jesus continues his work of salvation in the community currently. A perspicuous example of this is the healing of Peter's mother-in-law. Mark 1:29–30 tells of this incident as part of a visit to Capernaum. Jesus exerts power physically, actually taking the woman by the hand and lifting her up. Luke 4:38–39 has organized a sequence of exorcisms within the day's work at Capernaum and accordingly turns this healing into an exorcism in which Jesus "rebukes" the fever and "immedi-ately she rose and served them." The word "immediately" here represents a certain enhancement with respect to Mark: it heightens the wonder of the miracle. But Matthew 8:14–15 gives this healing a different narrative set-ting altogether as one of ten miracles following the Sermon on the Mount. He concentrates the story on Jesus alone, eliminating the secondary per-sonages and details. Jesus no longer needs to be told of the illness, nor is he beseeched to heal it. He simply "saw" the woman lying sick and "touched" her hand so that the fever left her, "and she rose and served him." Mark and Luke conclude that she served "them" (the disciples), but Matthew insists that she served *him*. This, in effect, simplifies the story to make the mother-in-law a symbol of the resurrected Church serving its glorified Lord.[6]

Similar tendencies in Matthew to sacrifice incidental narrative detail in order to more sharply focus the central significance of Christ for the Church can be documented by comparison of the synoptic accounts of the Stilling of the Storm (Matt 8:23–27; Mark 4:35–41; Luke 8:22–25). The dis-ciples are swamped by the waves in a violent tempest—σεισμὸς, suggesting

6. Such a parallel reading of this and other miracles in the synoptic Gospels is pro-posed by Étienne Charpentier, *Pour Lire Le Nouveau Testament*, where numerous other commonplaces of New Testament scholarship evoked in these pages are conveniently summarized.

a seismic eruption, which is symbolic of the end of the world. They wake and implore Jesus, saying, "Save, Lord; we are perishing." The Greek entreaty Κύριε σῶσον ("Save, Lord") was a liturgical formula in the early Church, very much like the Latin supplication *Kyrie eleison* ("Lord, have mercy"). It makes audible the Church's pleading for help and salvation. Matthew thus allows us to descry the contemporary experience of the early Church at worship beneath the narrative of Jesus's acts with his original disciples. The former is the experience out of which his narration arises and in which it remains embedded.

Such experience is the locus of religious truth experienced as always present in the revelation of Jesus as alive in the faith community and thus always the believer's contemporary: it makes the Gospel the perfect paradigm of a humanities text. The truth of such texts happens all over again, ever again, in the event of their reading and interpretation. In liturgy and worship, Jesus is revealed as the risen Lord and as with his Church always, "even unto the end of the world" (28:20).

One must experience Jesus in the present in order to believe in the truth of the Gospel story. It is especially the present experience of the death and resurrection of Jesus that remains the literally crucial event out of which the whole of the Gospel is conceived. This event and its being relived every day—*hodie resurrexit* ("He is risen today"), as the Easter liturgy has it—establishes the frame for the Gospel portrait of Jesus's life as a whole. The Easter event provides the key to reading this story as applying to one's own life and its possibility of becoming a resurrected life freed from every type of deadening "mortal" sin and mental slavery.

III. The Gospels Begin from Easter

As a testimony of faith in the risen Lord, the Gospels begin essentially from Easter. That is when the protagonist is finally revealed in his true identity and as establishing by open and incontrovertible signs the Kingdom of God. Previously, apart from exceptionally privileged moments, such as Peter's confession at Caesarea Philippi: "Thou art the Christ, the son of the living God" (Matt 16:13ff), this identity had been closely guarded as the "messianic secret."[7] Even after the revelation to Peter at Caesarea Philippi, the secret is reinstated immediately: "Then he sternly ordered his disciples not to tell anyone that he was the Messiah" (16:20). When asked why he speaks

7. Wrede, *Das Messiasgeheimnis*.

in parables in public, Jesus replies, "To you it has been given to know the se-
crets of the kingdom of heaven, but to them it has not been given" (13:11).
It is only with the Easter event, comprising Christ's death and resurrection,
followed up by Pentecost and the pouring out of the Spirit, that the good
news of Jesus Christ as the Son of God is ripe to be publicized beyond the
circle of his intimates and disciples. From that point forward, everything
is seen in a new light with the help of the Holy Spirit. Yet Matthew's whole
Gospel is written from precisely this point of view *after* the Christ event.
The Messianic secret so crucial to the drama that Mark creates is divulged
by Matthew, even if still only for those who have ears to hear and thus in
correlation with an inward condition.

The Easter experience is behind and within everything recounted by
Matthew even about Jesus's earthly existence: all the memories of him are
transfigured in the light of Easter. Upon Easter are leveraged not only the
New Testament's celebrations of the risen Christ and the preaching of salvation through him but also the narratives—especially Matthew's—about his
earlier life and mission: all point towards the Paschal mystery as the story's
climax and consummation.

Particularly significant, then, is the way that the Gospels represent the
Easter event itself narratively. There are basically two sets of images used
to express the mystery of Easter: Return to life and Ascension to glory. The
first is a before/after schema serving to affirm continuity between the earthly and the exalted Jesus. The second is a high/low schema emphasizing the
radical otherness of the resurrected life.[8] He is both the same Jesus come
back again (resurrected) and yet totally different because transfigured and
glorified (exalted). These are two complementary faces of the same mystery.

Matthew does not actually narrate any ascension, as do Luke (24:50–
53; cf. Acts 1:9–11) and Mark (16: 19, in the so-called Longer Ending), but
the apparition of Jesus after his resurrection in Matthew presents a glorified, perhaps already ascended Christ. In fact, seeing the resurrected Jesus
on the appointed mountain in Galilee already requires faith: "And when
they saw him, they worshipped him: but some doubted" (28:17). Neither
is he given fish to eat, as is the case in the other synoptic Gospels, in token
of his physicality prior to the Ascension. Instead, Jesus "came" (28:18) to
his disciples, even though they were already bowed down before him. Evidently, he "came" in some other sense besides the merely physical one, since
according to the narrative he is already standing there before them. As the

8. Cf. Charpentier, *Pour Lire Le Nouveau Testament*, 39.

one who comes, Jesus is assimilated to the Son of Man in Daniel, "who came with the clouds of heaven and came to the Ancient of Days" (7:13), and to Christ at the Second Coming as he is invoked at the end of the Book of Revelation ("Even so, come, Lord Jesus," 22:20).

Matthew portrays Jesus as he is in and for his Church. Matthew enables us to see not only the superimposition of the present experience of Christ in the faith community upon the past, the "history" of Jesus: he clearly brings out also the anticipation in the Church of the future fulfillment of the Kingdom that is to be definitively accomplished at Christ's Second Coming. It is already announced in Jesus's ministry—"The Kingdom of God is at hand"—and is actually inaugurated by the Easter event, as marked by the earthquake and the rending of the veil of the temple (27:51) along with other apocalyptic signs. Jesus's death is the beginning of the end of the world. His resurrection is the beginning of the Kingdom of God, as suggested by the *general* resurrection that commences with his death and resurrection. Thus, immediately after Jesus's death on the Cross and the attendant earthquake, "the graves were opened; and many bodies of saints which slept arose, and came out of the graves after his resurrection, and went into the holy city, and appeared unto many" (27:52–53). These are clear signs that the afterlife of the saints in New Jerusalem has already begun.

Matthew is the Gospel writer who actually develops the idea of the Church as an eschatological community, the Kingdom of God. The Gospel according to Mark, in its original form, breaks off abruptly with the Resurrection at 16:8. John is not interested in the historical Church. His Jesus says, "My kingdom is not of this world" (18:36). Luke reserves his ecclesiology for a second work, the Acts of the Apostles. Only at the very end of the Gospel according to Luke, at the breaking of bread, that is, in the celebration of the sacrament of the Eucharist, is Jesus recognized as the risen Lord by the pilgrims to Emmaus (24:13–35). But Matthew's Jesus stands all along in the light of Easter, in which the glorified Lord is recognized and worshipped by his community. The Easter event is apocalyptic and casts present life, the daily life of the Church, in the light of the end-time.

If Easter guides the story all along, the Resurrection is really where the Gospel of the Kingdom begins. But this is to say, again, that the Gospel begins with faith, for to perceive the resurrected Jesus requires faith. This is evident even at Jesus's final appearance on the mountain in Galilee, where some doubted (28:17). This difference among witnesses implies that the

Gospel revelation is not a wholly objective event; it depends instead on how different individuals perceive and receive it. The miracle takes place, at the deepest level, inside people and manifests itself in the transformation of their lives. The *physical* healing, for example, of the two blind men in Matthew 9:27–30 is added as a *sign* of the *spiritual* recovery of sight accomplished already in their acceptance of Jesus as Savior: "According to your faith be it unto you" (see also 9:1–8), as Jesus tells them. Prophecy in general works this way—not by imposing an inevitable fate or solid fact, but by inviting to the realization of possibilities of life through interpreting the past in the freedom of the present with a view to the future that it can make possible. The Gospels in this perspective are paradigmatic for humanities texts as calling to be constantly re-actualized: they live a resurrected life themselves in each successive age. They are animated by being appropriated and lived anew, thanks to interpretations in which their potential for truth is newly tapped into and revealed.

These select observations on the Gospel according to Matthew have been offered in an attempt to give some sense of how the Gospels represent a consummate work of interpretation, where the facts of Jesus's life are recounted not for their own sake, but as a testimonial of faith and for the purpose of revealing an overarching order of significance, a providential plan for history and redemption. As such, moreover, the Gospel works as interpellation—it calls all who hear to conversion of life in light of the truth it discloses. Near the end of his Gospel, John states explicitly that everything in it is written to the end that its hearers or readers might believe "that Jesus is the Christ, the Son of God; and that believing ye might have life through his name" (20:31). Beyond this common purpose, the differences between the various Gospels highlight how different writers and communities inflect and nuance the Gospel message in ways reflecting their own cultures and concerns. Precisely this variability according to context serves to reveal a meaning that is not limited to any one historical moment but rather transcends its own time and is prophetic. Like prophetic works generally, the Gospels reveal the end of history, its ultimate destination and purpose. Of course, they do so always from within specific historical limits, and yet as if these limits were miraculously suspended.

CONCLUSION

The Bible as Exemplary Humanities Text

THE GOSPELS READ IN this way (as in the immediately preceding chapter) are miraculous and extraordinary, and yet they turn out to be exemplary of humanities texts and their potential to become life-transforming and world-revealing. This has actually been the case for each of the biblical books and literary genres that have been inventoried in the course of this condensed survey with its textual samplings. All of these genres, in some manner, are summed up and recapitulated in the Gospel. Taken together, these generically diverse works represent the ideal of a Book speaking with authority and disclosing a truth that can serve as guide for human beings living in the present. This guidance orients humans to a comprehensive outlook on the universe, one reaching beyond their finite capacities of knowing.

As such, typically, the Bible is set apart from profane works by human beings, but it is also possible to see the Bible as realizing this miraculous potential exemplarily. Its revelatory power in some sense inheres in the capacity of literary works in general for expressing sublime imaginations that enable humans to relate to the infinite and whole and to register intimations pushing up against the limits of the invisible and unrepresentable. Theology offers an eminent discourse for interpreting this reality that extends beyond the range of representation and finitude and yet determines everything in our concrete existence.

We do not know what human beings are capable of, certainly not until their capacities to reach out for and to receive the divine have been fully deployed and exploited. Is it because the biblical books are so powerful and poignant as literature that they are revelatory of the ends of human life and the world—of our highest ideals and most enticing imaginings? Or is it their unaccountably divine and revelatory power that makes them so compelling as literature? In either case, secular literature, too, in its technical capabilities and ingenuity, can show up as transfigured by the light of theological revelation. Theological imagination renders explicit the potentially inspired status of imagination as such when taken to its own putative limits and employed even beyond them. Its powers of self-transcendence are not necessarily only its own but may also be received, in wondering and humbling thankfulness, as gifts from a wholly (holy) Other.

In this monograph, I have taken the Bible, which is traditionally viewed as sacred Word and revelation, and have read it on the basis of its resources as literature. I have done so not in order to translate the sacred into the secular but rather to reveal the potential of the presumably secular—in this instance, literary creation, which in our modern culture generally counts as worldly and human—for disclosing and incarnating the sacred and thus for achieving a theological vision and revelation. "Theological revelation" here means disclosure of a comprehensive significance for the world and of an ultimate meaning for human life—through reference to figures of divinity. This register of meaning must be taken to heart and be enacted in order to become true to life. To flourish, such meaning cannot remain purely abstract but must be lived out in flesh and in spirit. Such a disclosure may be imagined as coming directly and necessarily from God, but in any case one must invest oneself in it by believing it in order to make it come true. Revelation in this sense entails receptiveness to what exceeds our rational and imaginative powers—yet only as their own intrinsic source rather than as an alien force. Hence the figure of a Creator typically serves to symbolize a relation of dependence on and belonging to what or Who transcends one and nonetheless also enables one's every act and expression of self—indeed one's very existence itself.

My theological and critical reflection has interpreted the Bible as revelation, as Word of God, but it has done so not by mystifying this book's nature as wholly other to all other books classed as products of merely human hands. Instead, the Bible has been taken as exemplary, as opening to view some of the furthest and fullest possibilities of what literature can be at its highest and most inspired. This does not make Holy Scripture exclusively the product of human beings; instead, it reveals the work of humans as potentially directed by and toward the infinite and unknowable, toward what in theology (especially negative theology) is interpreted as divinity. Divinization, as an eminent goal to which human aspiration can be oriented, emerges here as an imaginable destiny. It is realized, among other ways, through literary endeavor understood as the work of human invention and creativity—but also projected as entailing a kind of consecration conferred via a vocation to the cult of letters. This striving and aspiring toward a transcendent ideal understood as a God who grants and graces this very impulse itself is what I propose as witness to a theology of literature that is revealed in and through the Bible read in the tradition of the humanities.

Bibliographical Note to Conclusion

The phenomenology of human receptiveness and divine reciprocity in the context of biblical revelation is examined penetratingly by Abraham Heschel in *Die Prophetie* (1936) and in *Prophetic Inspiration after the Prophets: Maimonides and Other Medieval Authorities* (1996). Heschel calls these two complementary movements "theotropic" and "anthropotropic," respectively. I develop in detail the negative-theological underpinnings of such an argument in *Poetry and Apocalypse*, Part 1: "A Critical Negative Theology of Poetic Language."

Bibliography

Agar, Jolyon. *Post-Secularism, Realism and Utopia: Transcendence and Immanence from Hegel to Bloch*. New York: Routledge, 2014.

Aletti, J. N., and J. L. Ska, eds. *Biblical Exegesis in Progress*. Rome: Istituto Pontificio, 2009.

Alkier, Stefan, and Richard B. Hays, eds. *Die Bibel im Dialog der Schriften: Konzepte intertextueller Bibellektüre*. Tübingen/Basel: A. Francke, 2005. Translated as *Reading the Bible Intertextually*. Waco, TX: Baylor University Press, 2009.

Alter, Robert. *The Art of Biblical Narrative*. New York: Basic Books, 1981.

——. *The Art of Biblical Poetry*. New York: Basic Books, 1985.

Alter, Robert, and Frank Kermode, eds. *The Literary Guide to the Bible*. Cambridge: Harvard University Press, 1987.

Anderson, Bernard W., ed. *Out of the Depths: The Psalms Speak for us Today*. 3rd ed. Philadelphia: Westminster, 2000.

Anderson, Gary A. *The Genesis of Perfection: Adam and Eve in Jewish and Christian Imagination*. Louisville: Westminster John Knox, 2001.

Assmann, Jan. *Das kulturelle Gedächtnis: Schrift, Erinnerung und politische Identität in frühen Hochkulturen*. Translated as *Cultural Memory and Early Civilization: Writing, Remembrance, and Political Imagination*. Cambridge University Press, 2011.

Bal, Mieke. *Loving Yusuf: Conceptual Travels from Present to Past*. Chicago: University of Chicago Press, 2008.

Bhabha, Homi K., ed. *Nation and Narration*. New York: Routledge, 1990.

Benjamin, Walter. *Angelus Novus: Ausgewählte Schriften*. Translated by Harry Zohn as *Illuminations*. New York: Schocken, 1969.

——. *Einbahnstraße*. Berlin: Rowohlt, 1928.

Blake, William. *The Complete Poetry and Prose of William Blake*. Ed. David W. Erdman. Berkeley: University of California Press, 1982.

Blond, Phillip, ed. *Post-Secular Philosophy: Between Philosophy and Theology*. London: Routledge, 1998.

Bloom, Harold, ed. *The Book of J*. Translated by David Rosenberg. New York: Grove Weidenfeld, 1990.

Boitani, Piero. *Ri–scritture*. Translated by Anita Weston as *The Bible and its Rewritings*. Oxford: Oxford University Press, 1999.

Brown, Raymond E. *The Birth of the Messiah: A Commentary on the Infancy Narratives in the Gospels of Matthew and Luke.* New York: Doubleday, 1999.

Brueggemann, Walter. *An Introduction to the Old Testament: The Canon and Christian Imagination.* Louisville: Westminster John Knox, 2003.

———. *The Prophetic Imagination*, 2nd ed. Minneapolis: Fortress, 2001.

———. *Texts Under Negotiation: The Bible and Postmodern Imagination.* Minneapolis: Augsburg, 1994.

———. *Theology of the Old Testament: Testimony, Dispute, Advocacy.* Minneapolis: Fortress, 2005.

Buber, Martin. *Moses: The Revelation and the Covenant.* New York: Harper & Row, 1958.

———. *On the Bible: Eighteen Studies.* New York: Schocken, 1968.

Bultmann, Rudolph. *Theologie des Neuen Testaments*, 9th ed. Translated by Kendrick Grobel as *Theology of the New Testament*. New York: Scribner, 1955.

Campbell, Antony F., and Mark A. O'Brien. *Sources of the Pentateuch: Texts, Introductions, Annotations.* Minneapolis: Fortress, 1993.

Carruthers, Jo, Mark Knight, and Andrew Tate, eds. *Literature and the Bible: A Reader.* London: Routledge, 2014.

Charpentier, Étienne. *Pour Lire L'ancien Testament.* Paris: Cerf, 1983.

———. *Pour Lire Le Nouveau Testament.* Paris: Cerf, 1981.

Chrétien, Jean-Louis. *Symbolique du corps: La tradition chrétienne du Cantique des Cantiques.* Paris: Presses Universitaires de France, 2005.

Crossan, John Dominic. *The Historical Jesus: The Life of a Mediterranean Jewish Peasant.* San Francisco: Harper & Row, 1991.

Damrosch, David. *The Narrative Covenant: Transformations of Genre in the Growth of Biblical Literature.* San Francisco: Harper and Row, 1987.

Dibelius, Martin. *Die Formgeschichte des Evangeliums.* Translated by Bertram Lee Woolf as *From Tradition to Gospel*. Cambridge: J. Clarke, 1971.

Eckhart, Meister. *Meister Eckhart: The Essential Sermons, Commentaries, Treatises, and Defense.* Translated by Edmond Colledge and Bernard McGinn. New York: Paulist, 1981.

Eslin, Jean-Claude, ed. *La Bible: 2000 Ans de Lectures.* Paris: Desclée de Brouwer, 2003.

Falk, Marcia. *Love Lyrics from the Bible: A Translation and Literary Study of the Song of Songs.* Sheffield: Almond, 1982.

Firth, David G., and Jamie A. Grant, eds. *Words & the Word: Explorations in Biblical Interpretation & Literary Theory.* Downers Grove, IL: InterVarsity, 2008.

Franke, William. "The Linguistic Turning of the Symbol: Baudelaire and his French Symbolist Heirs." In *Baudelaire and the Poetics of Modernity,* edited by Patricia Ward. Nashville: Vanderbilt University Press, 2000.

———. "Involved Knowing: On the Poetic Epistemology of the Humanities." *Humanities* 4.4 (2015) 600–22.

———. *Poetry and Apocalypse: Theological Disclosures of Poetic Language.* Stanford: Stanford University Press, 2009.

———. *The Revelation of Imagination: From Homer and the Bible through Virgil and Augustine to Dante.* Evanston, IL: Northwestern University Press, 2015.

———. *Secular Scriptures: Modern Theological Poetics in the Wake of Dante.* Columbus: Ohio State University Press, 2016.

Frei, Hans W. *The Eclipse of Biblical Narrative: A Study in Eighteenth and Nineteenth Century Hermeneutics.* New Haven: Yale University Press, 1974.

Fretheim, Terrence E., and Karlfried Froehlich. *The Bible as Word of God in a Postmodern Age*. Minneapolis: Fortress Press, 1998.

Friedman, Richard Elliott. *The Bible with Sources Revealed: A View into the Five Books of Moses*. San Francisco: Harper SanFrancisco, 2003.

Frisch, Harold. *Poetry with a Purpose: Biblical Poetics and Interpretation*. Bloomington: Indiana University Press, 1988.

Frye, Northrop. *Anatomy of Criticism: Four Essays*. Princeton: Princeton University Press, 1957.

———. *The Double Vision: Language and Meaning in Religion*. Toronto: University of Toronto Press, 1991.

———. *The Great Code: The Bible and Literature*. New York: Harcourt Brace Jovanovich, 1981.

Gertz, Jan Christian, Konrad Schmid, and Markus Witte, eds. *Abschied vom Jawisten: Die Komposition des Hexateuch in der jüngsten Diskussion*. Berlin: Walter de Gruyter, 2002.

Goodman, Lenn E. *Islamic Humanism*. Oxford: Oxford University Press, 2003.

Gunkel, Hermann. *Einleitung in die Psalmen: Die Gattungen der religiösen Lyrik Israels*. Translated by James Nogalski as *Introduction to Psalms: The Genres of the Religious Lyric of Israel*. Macon, GA: Mercer University Press, 1993.

———. *Die Propheten*. Göttingen: Vandenhoeck & Ruprecht, 1917.

Habermas, Jürgen. *Ein Bewußtsein von dem, was fehlt: eine Diskussion mit Jürgen Habermas*. Edited by Michale Reder and Josef Schmidt. Frankfurt a.M.: Suhrkamp, 2008. Translated by Ciaran Cronin as *An Awareness of What Is Missing: Faith and Reason in a Post-Secular Age*. Cambridge, UK: Polity, 2010.

Heschel, Abraham Joshua. "The Holy Dimension." *Journal of Religion* 23 (1943) 117–24

———. *Prophetic Inspiration after the Prophets: Maimonides and Other Medieval Authorities*. Edited by Morris M. Faierstein. Hoboken, NJ: Ktav, 1996.

———. *The Prophets*. Peabody, MA: Prince, 2003.

Hunt, Patrick. *Poetry in the Song of Songs: A Literary Analysis*. New York: Peter Lang, 2008.

Irigaray, Luce. *Éthique de la différence sexuelle*. Paris: Éditions de Minuit, 1984.

Jacobson, Douglas and Rhonda Hustedt Jacobson, eds. *The American University in a Postsecular Age*. New York: Oxford University Press, 2008.

Jasper, David and Stephen Prickett, eds. *The Bible and Literature: A Reader*. Oxford: Blackwell, 1999.

Kass, Leon R. *The Beginning of Wisdom: Reading Genesis*. Chicago: University of Chicago Press, 2003.

Kristeva, Julia. *La révolution du langage poetique*. Paris: Seuil, 1974.

Kugel, James L. *In Potiphar's House: The Interpretive Life of Biblical Texts*. San Francisco: Harper San Francisco, 1990.

Leavitt, John, ed. *Poetry and Prophecy: The Anthropology of Inspiration*. Ann Arbor: University of Michigan Press, 1997.

Lemon, Rebecca, Christine Joynes, Emma Masson, Jonathan Roberts, and Christopher Rowland, eds. *The Blackwell Companion to the Bible in English Literature*. Oxford: Blackwell, 2009.

Lincoln, Bruce. *Discourse and the Construction of Society: Comparative Studies of Myth, Ritual, and Classification*. New York: Oxford University Press, 1989.

Lubac, Henri de. *L'éxégèse médiévale: Les quatre sens de l'écriture*. Translated by E. M. Macierowski as *Medieval Exegesis*, 4 vols. Grand Rapids: Erdmans, 1998.

May, Herbert G., and Bruce M. Metzger, eds. *The Oxford Annotated Bible*. New York: Oxford University Press, 1962.

McEntire, Mark. *Struggling With God: An Introduction to the Pentateuch*. Macon: Mercer University Press, 2009.

McGrath, Alister E. *In the Beginning: The Story of the King James Bible and How it Changed a Nation, a Language, and a Culture*. New York: Doubleday, 2001.

Meier, John P. *Jesus: A Marginal Jew. Rethinking the Historical Jesus*. New York: Doubleday, 1991.

Miller, J. Hillis. "Parable and Performative in the Gospels and in Modern Literature." *Tropes, Parables and Performatives*. Hertfordshire: Harvester Wheatsheaf, 1991.

Montemaggi, Vittorio, and Thomas Treherne, eds. *Dante's Commedia: Theology as Poetry*. Notre Dame: Notre Dame University Press, 2010.

———. *Divinity Realized in Human Encounter: Reading Dante's* Commedia *as Theology*. Oxford: Oxford University Press, 2016.

Mowinckel, Sigmund. *The Psalms in Israel's Worship*. Trans. Dafydd Rhys AP-Thomas. Oxford: Blackwell, 1962. Originally *Psalmenstudien*. Oslo: J. Dybwad, 1921.

Niehaus, Jeffrey J. *Ancient Near Eastern Themes in Biblical Theology*. Grand Rapids: Kregal, 2008.

Noth, Martin. *Überlieferungsgeschichte des Pentateuch*. Translated by B. W. Anderson as *A History of Pentateuchal Traditions*. Englewood Cliffs, NJ: Prentice-Hall, 1972.

Pagels, Elaine. *Adam, Eve, and the Serpent*. New York: Random, 1988.

Pelletier, Anne–Marie. *Lectures du Cantique des Cantiques: De l'énigme du sens aux figures du lecteur*. Rome: Editrice Pontificio Biblico, 1989.

Petersen, David L., ed. *Prophecy in Israel: Search for an Identity*. Philadelphia: Fortress, 1987.

Plastras, James C. M., *The God of Exodus: The Theology of the Exodus Narratives*. Milwaukee: Bruce, 1966.

Polanyi, Michael. *Personal Knowledge. Towards a Post-Critical Philosophy*. London: Routledge, 1998.

Ransom, Emily A., ed., with Peter Hawkins. "Rethinking the Bible as Literature: A Pedagogical Forum." *Religion and Literature* 47/1 (2015): 170-242.

Reed, Walter L. *Dialogues of the Word: The Bible as Literature According to Bakhtin*. Oxford: Oxford University Press, 1993.

Renaud, Bernard. *La théophanie du Sinai: Ex 19–24*. Paris: J. Gabalda, 1991.

Richards. I. A. *The Philosophy of Rhetoric*. Oxford: Oxford University Press, 1965.

Ricoeur, Paul. *Essays on Biblical Interpretation*. Edited by Lewis S. Mudge. Philadelphia: Fortress, 1980.

———. *Figuring the Sacred: Religion, Narrative, and Imagination*. Philadelphia: Fortress, 1995.

———. *Interpretation Theory: Discourse and the Surplus of Meaning*. Fort Worth: Texas Christian University Press, 1976.

Ricoeur, Paul, and André Lacoque. *Thinking Biblically: Exegetical and Hermeneutical Studies*. Chicago: University of Chicago Press, 1998.

Robert, A. "Le genre littéraire du Cantique des Cantiques." *Revue biblique* 52 (1943–44) 192–213.

Roskies, David G. *Against Apocalypse: Responses to Catastrophe in Modern Jewish Culture*. Cambridge: Harvard University Press, 1984.

Sarna, Nahum M. *On the Book of Psalms: Exploring the Prayers of Ancient Israel.* New York: Schocken, 1993.

———. *Songs of the Heart: An Introduction to the Book of Psalms.* New York: Schocken, 1993.

Schökel, Luis Alonso. "Isaiah." In *The Literary Guide to the Bible,* edited by Robert Alter and Frank Kermode, 165–83. Cambridge: Harvard University Press, 1999.

Schwartz, Regina, ed. *The Book and the Text: The Bible and Literary Theory.* Oxford: Blackwell, 1990.

Schweitzer, Albert. *The Quest for the Historical Jesus: A Critical Study of Its Progress from Reimarus to Wrede.* Translated by W. Montgomery. London: A. & C. Black, 1910.

Seow, C. L. *Job 1–21: Interpretation and Commentary.* Grand Rapids: Eerdemans, 2013.

Spinks, D. Christopher. *The Bible and the Crisis of Meaning: Debates on the Theological Meaning of Scripture.* London: T. & T. Clark, 2007.

Strauss, David Friedrich. *Das Leben Jesu, kritisch bearbeitet,* 2 vols. Translated by George Eliot as *The Life of Jesus Critically Examined.* London: Tübingen, 1846.

Tacey, David. *Religion as Metaphor: Beyond Literal Belief.* New Brunswick: Transaction, 2014.

Taylor, Charles. *A Secular Age.* Cambridge: Harvard Belknap, 2007.

Thompson, Leonard L. *Introducing Biblical Literature: A More Fantastic Country.* Englewood Cliffs, NJ: Prentice–Hall, 1998.

Tronk, Mendel W. *Wesen und Ursprung der Sprache: Eine Untersuchung.* Berlin: Frieling, 1995.

Vermeylen, Jacques. *Du prophète Isaïe à l'apocalyptique: Isaïe, I–XXXV,* 2 vols. Paris: J. Gabalda, 1977–78.

Voegelin, Eric. *Israel and Revelation.* Baton Rouge: Louisiana State University Press, 1956.

von Rad, Gerhard. *Theologie des Alten Testaments.* Translated by D. M. G. Stalker as *Old Testament Theology: The Theology of Israel's Historical Traditions.* Louisville: Westminster John Knox, 2001.

Warner, Marina. *Alone of All Her Sex: The Myth and the Cult of the Virgin Many.* 2nd ed. Oxford: Oxford University Press, 2013.

Wellhausen, Julius. *Prolegomena zur Geschichte Israels,* 1878.

Westermann, Claus. *Ausgewählte Psalmen.* Göttingen: Vandenhoeck & Ruprecht, 1984.

Wilder, Amos N. *The Bible and the Literary Critic.* Minneapolis: Fortress, 1991.

Winnett, F. V. *The Mosaic Tradition.* Toronto: University of Toronto Press, 1949.

Wrede, William. *Das Messiasgeheimnis in den Evangelien.* Translated by J. C. G. Greig as *The Messianic Secret.* Cambridge: J. Clarke, 1971.